Second Edition REVISED & EXPANDED

Making Furniture & Dollhouses

for American Girl® and Other 18-Inch Dolls

Acknowledgments

Producing a book requires the cooperative efforts of many people. I want to thank my family for forgiving my neglect during the many months it took to produce this book. I want to thank my daughter, Jill Kennedy, for the many hours spent converting my sketches into quality computer drawings for this book. I wish to thank my wife, Dena, for her editorial assistance and project design review. Thanks to the staff at Fox Chapel for their assistance and for giving me the opportunity to develop this book. Thanks to all customers who purchase this book—I hope you enjoy making the projects.

Publisher's Cataloging-in-Publication Data

Simmons, Dennis (Dennis Lee), 1950-

Making furniture & dollhouses for American Girl and other 18-inch dolls / by Dennis Simmons. -- Rev. & expanded ed. -- East Petersburg, PA : Fox Chapel Pub. Co., c2009.

p. ; cm.

ISBN: 978-1-56523-402-4
Rev. ed. of the author's: Making doll furniture in wood. c2004.

1. Doll furniture--Patterns. 2. Dollhouses--Patterns. 3.Woodwork--Patterns. I. Simmons, Dennis (Dennis Lee), 1950- . Making doll furniture in wood. II. Title.

TT175.5 .S56 2009
745.592/3--dc22   2009

Second Edition REVISED & EXPANDED

Making Furniture & Dollhouses

for American Girl® and Other 18-Inch Dolls

By Dennis Simmons

FOX CHAPEL
PUBLISHING

Contents

Using this Book 6

Dollhouse 11
    Historical American Houses 22

Chairs 35
    Rocking Chair 36
    Dining Chair 48
    Adirondack Chair 55
    Chair Desk 61

Tables 69
    Adirondack Table 70
    Dining Table 73
    Picnic Table 77
    Southwestern Nightstand 81

Beds 84
    Canopy Bed 85
    Bunk Bed 93
    Southwestern Bed 97
    Classic Bed 102

Dressers & Chests 108
    Tall Dresser 109
    Short Dresser 118
    Armoire 126
    Treasure Chest 135

Accessories 138
    Bookcase 139
    Grandfather Clock 142
    Mirror 151
    School Desk 159

Storage Cases 166
    Hope Chest 167
    Southwestern Trunk 174
    Traveling Case 180
    Classic Trunk 186

Appendix: Materials and Techniques 195

Using this Book

Dollhouse, page 11

I have enjoyed the challenge of designing and creating the furniture projects for this book. Furniture items have been designed to encompass a variety of cultures and time periods. The authentic furniture items are scaled to proportion for the 18" dolls that are so popular with children. These projects are designed to permit the craftperson to construct heirloom-quality furniture. All projects in this book could become treasured gifts for a daughter or granddaughter. I also envision these items proudly displaying a cherished doll handed down from a loved one. These furniture projects are created with the craftperson in mind. Each project is presented in a detailed step-by-step process from start to finish. The book includes simpler projects for the beginning woodworker, as well as more challenging projects for the advanced woodworker. All projects can be constructed using tools commonly found in home workshops. You can make chairs, tables, beds, dressers, chests, desks—even a mirror and bookcase for your 18" doll. Create a matching set of furniture in the classic, Victorian, Adirondack, or Southwestern styles. Additional pieces are included to showcase other types of furniture and decoration options.

Additionally, this revised and expanded edition features plans for a modular dollhouse—make one room or ten. I've also included instructions for customizing the look of the dollhouse to match different historical time periods. This way, you can collaborate with your child to make the dollhouse truly personal and special to them. Every child loves to imagine themselves as characters from their favorite books and movies. By involving your child in the design, they can choose the house they want—whether Anne of Green Gables, Sarah Plain and Tall, Laura Ingalls, Tom Sawyer, or a historical figure will be the eventual inhabitant.

I enjoyed creating this book and hope you enjoy making the projects.

Dennis Simmons
intarsiawood@hotmail.com

A dollhouse big enough for her dolls to play in is the dream of every doll-owner. This modular dollhouse enables you to make and stack as many rooms as you want, creating a shape to fit the space you have available. The tiny shingles, clapboard, delicate shutters, and see-through windows will amaze the lucky girl who receives one of these dollhouses. Additionally, versatile instructions are included to create a basic or highly customized dollhouse for each of the historic American Girl dolls. The best-known series of 18-inch dolls are those made by American Girl. For ease of cross-reference to these popular books and dolls, I've included information on each architectural style to help you choose if building around a particular series. The text shows you what you need to know to create basic and detailed dollhouses for each character. Create a tepee for Kaya, an adobe rancho for Josefina, a log home for Kirsten, a Victorian mansion for Samantha, and more.

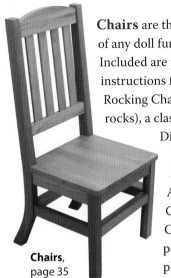

Chairs are the foundation of any doll furniture set. Included are plans and instructions for creating the Rocking Chair (which really rocks), a classic and simple Dining Chair (pictured), a miniature Adirondack Chair, and a Chair Desk—perfect for playing school.

Chairs, page 35

Tables create an area for dolls to entertain. Imagine your favorite girl helping her doll serve lemonade on the rustic Adirondack Table, a turkey dinner on the Dining Table, an outdoor barbeque on the Picnic Table (pictured), or a simple bedtime snack on the Southwestern Nightstand.

Tables, page 69

Beds are a great place for girls to host sleepover parties for their dolls. Choose from the fairy-tale Canopy Bed, the double-decker Bunk Bed (pictured), the geometric Southwestern Bed, or the simple Classic Bed.

Beds, page 84

Dressers and chests are the ideal accessory for a doll with lots of treasures to store. The doll handler in your life will appreciate the small drawers of the Tall Dresser and Short Dresser, the tiny hangers that go with the Armoire (pictured), and the storage space offered by the Treasure Chest.

Dressers & Chests, page 108

Accessories are necessary details for rounding out every furniture set. Whether your dollhouse needs a simple Bookcase, beautiful Grandfather Clock, delicate Mirror (pictured), or Victorian School Desk, you'll find the instructions here.

Accessories, page 138

Storage cases are furniture items in which to store the dolls themselves for safekeeping and travel. Your dolls will be kept safe and sound, whether you choose to build the elegant walnut Hope Chest, the rustic Southwestern Trunk, the sturdy Traveling Case, or the beautifully simple Classic Trunk (pictured).

Storage Cases, page 166

This picturesque bedroom suite provides a perfect play area. The drawers open and close, and the glass in the mirror is non-breakable.

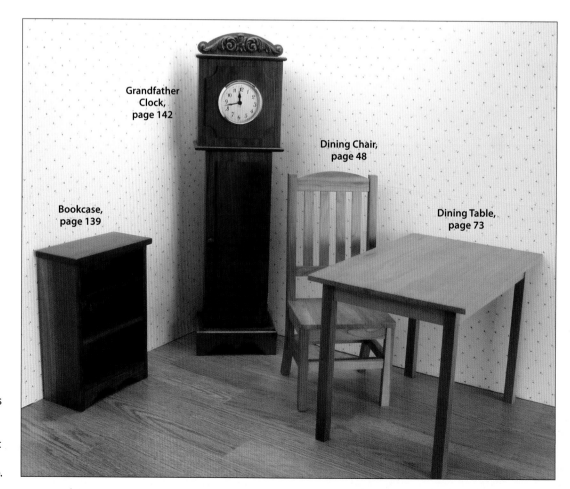

The focal point of this simple dining room set is the stately Grandfather Clock in the corner. The front of the clock cabinet opens and a working timepiece graces the top.

An Adirondack chair and table and a picnic table make a great outdoor set. Keep the planks small to provide a more scaled look.

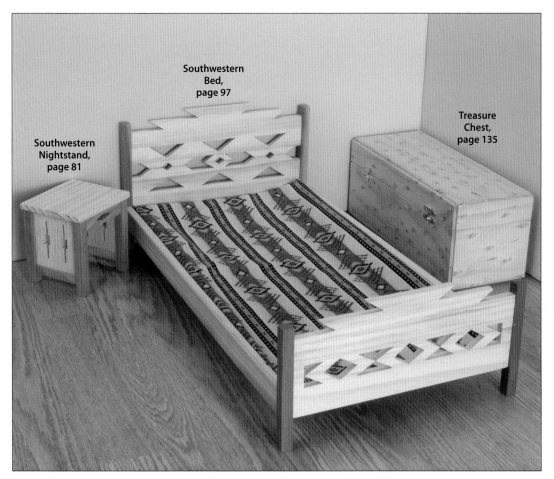

Angled cuts created with a scroll saw give this bedroom suite a Southwestern charm. Wood with a small grain pattern helps to give the furniture a realistic look.

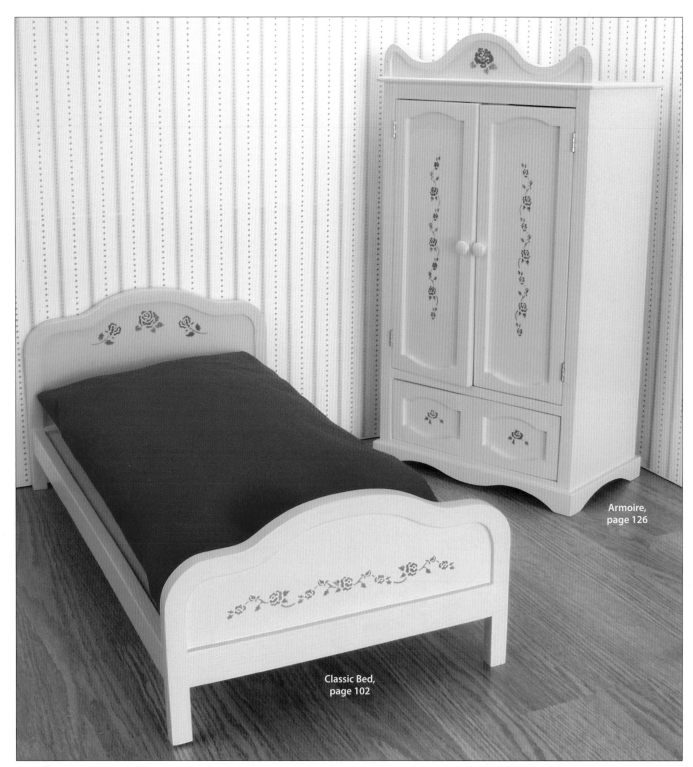

Armoire,
page 126

Classic Bed,
page 102

Any of the furniture in this book can be painted. Here, yellow acrylic paint and stenciled roses adorn a classic bedroom set. The doors of the armoire open to reveal a hanging rod.

Dollhouse

This modular dollhouse can be made of one room or multiple rooms to fit the play space available. A single room is 24" x 36", large enough to accommodate the furniture shown in this book. A second story could be added below by making additional walls and floor sections.

To make this dollhouse, you will need ½" thick medium-density fiberboard (MDF), a material commonly available at your local home center or lumber store. MDF costs less than plywood, does not have a grain direction, and is easily cut and painted.

Directions to customize the dollhouse in historic styles are included beginning on page 22. Follow the lists to discover the elements needed for each home, then follow the instructions to create each individual element.

To assemble the dollhouse, first place the floor where desired, grooves up. Then place the long back wall into the groove. Place the end walls. Finally, commission a helper to position the roof. Place the upper end of the roof in contact with the end walls first, then carefully lower the roof while aligning the tongue and groove.

An optional green space on the outside of the house can accommodate landscape plants cut on the scroll saw or purchased at a hobby craft store.

Dollhouse

Shingles

Gingerbread Trim

Clapboard

Shutters

Windows

Corner Trim

Clapboard

Cut ⅛" hardboard sheet material into 1½" wide strips. Install the clapboard with a 1¼" reveal. Use a little construction adhesive along the lap line, then place a few pin nails along the top edge of each piece. A pneumatic nail gun with ½"-long 23 gauge headless pin nails can be used for this task. Cut and install pieces of wood to form the corner trim.

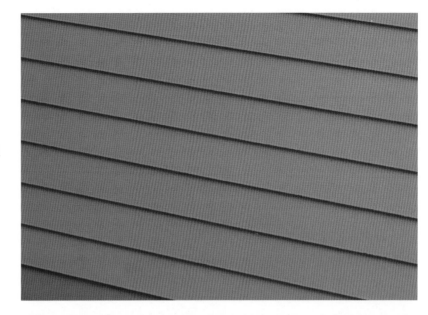

Gingerbread trim

The gingerbread trim along the eaves adds a decorative touch. Drill a series of holes into the wood strip with a ⅜" bit. The centers of the holes are about ¾" apart. A notch is cut to form the arrowhead design.

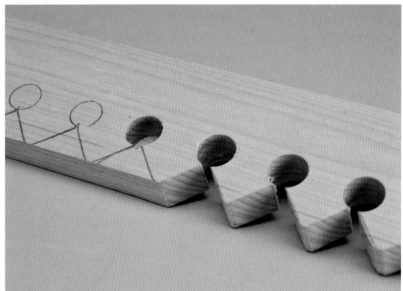

Shingles

Rip-cut ⅛" thick strips of cedar into 1¾" long pieces and fasten using a 1¼" reveal. Use construction adhesive and a ½"-long pin nail for each shingle.

Shutters

Cut shutters from ¼"-thick wood into 10¼" x 3¾" rectangles. The oval inside is 8¼" tall and 2¼" wide. Make the three sunrays in each corner by drilling a large hole with a ⅜" drill bit and a smaller hole with a ⅛" drill bit. Use a scroll saw to cut between the two circles to create the ray.

Rectangular Windows

Cut window sashes from ⅛"-thick wood. The exterior rectangle should be 10¼" x 7⅜". The interior rectangle should be 8⅛" x 5⅜". Paint as desired. Attach the frames with pin nails and adhesive. The window openings are cut through in the end walls with a jigsaw to provide a creative play opportunity. The window in the back wall is not visible from the interior to permit more flexible furniture arrangement.

Corner Trim

Create corner trim by cutting a tongue and groove joint.

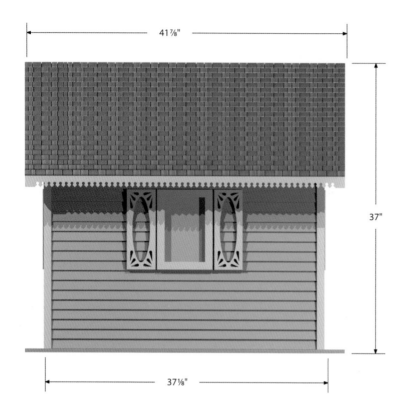

41⅞"

37⅛"

37"

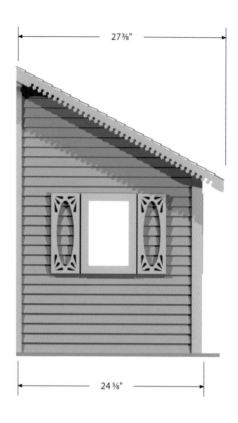

27⅜"

24⅝"

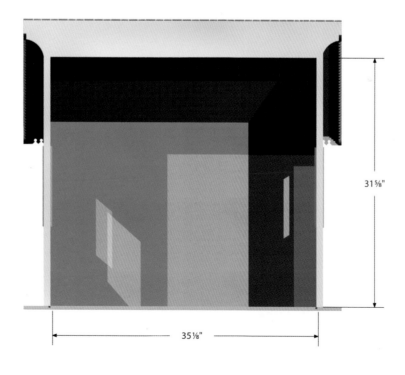

31⅝"

35⅛"

Assembly Drawing

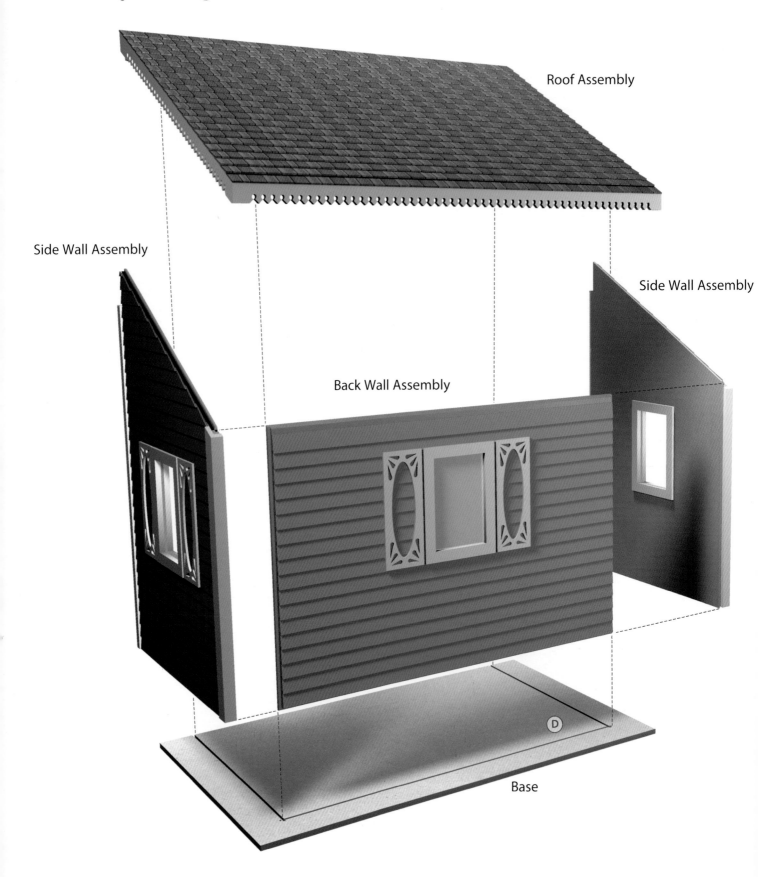

Roof Assembly

Side Wall Assembly

Side Wall Assembly

Back Wall Assembly

D

Base

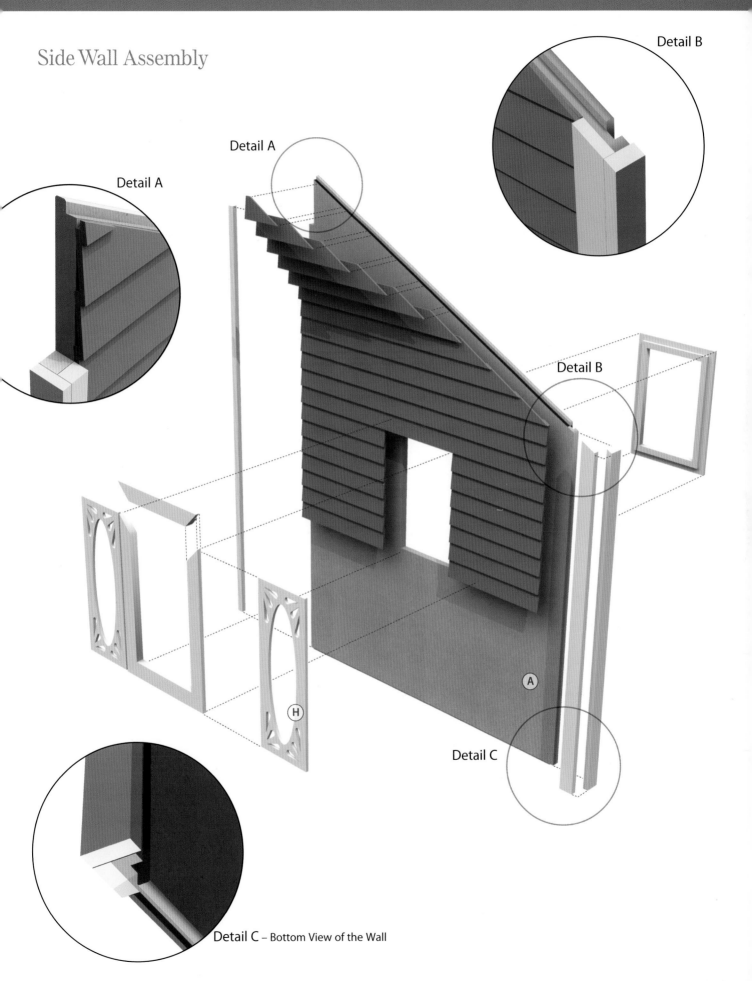

Side Wall Assembly

Detail A

Detail A

Detail B

Detail B

Detail C

Detail C – Bottom View of the Wall

Back Wall Assembly

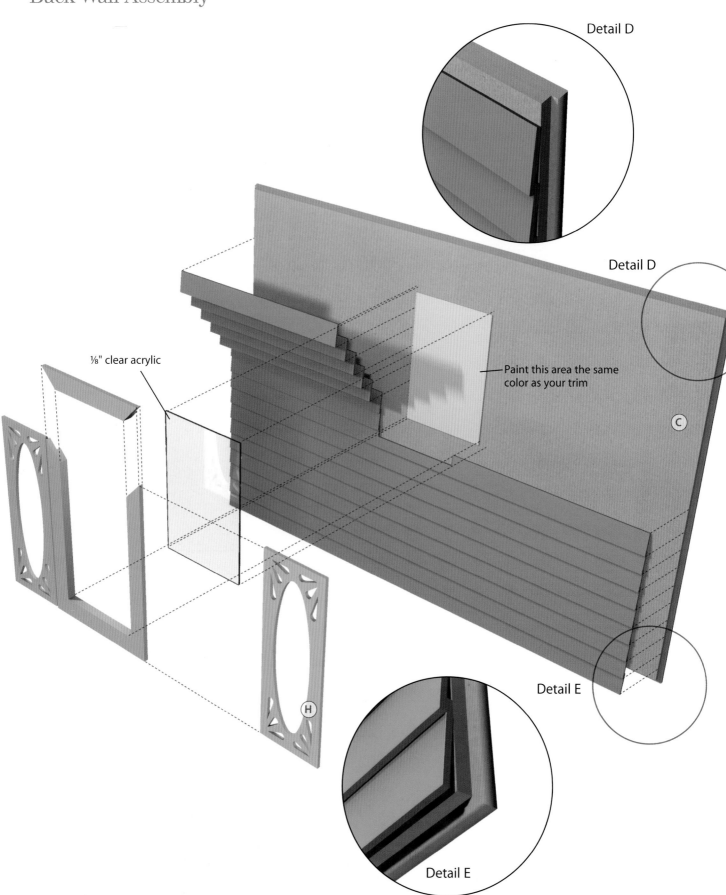

Detail D

Detail D

⅛" clear acrylic

Paint this area the same color as your trim

C

H

Detail E

Detail E

Roof Assembly

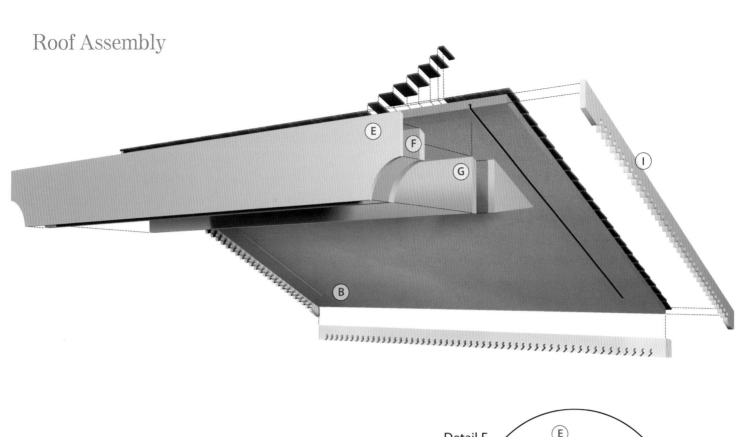

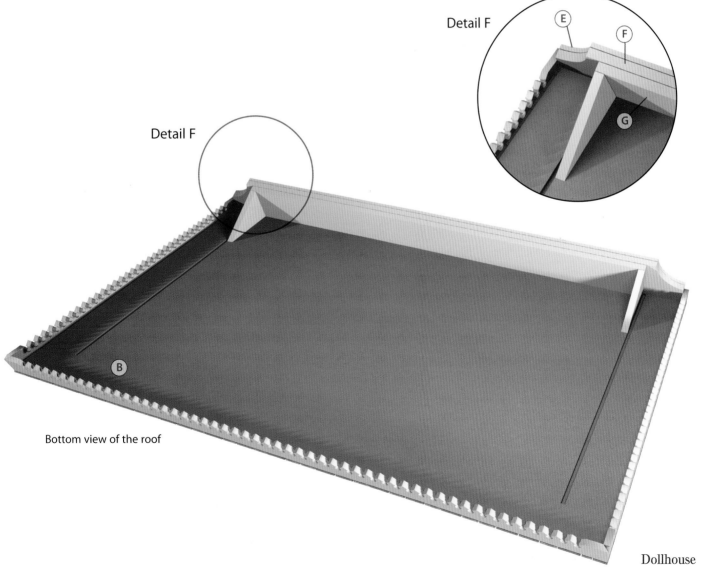

Detail F

Detail F

Bottom view of the roof

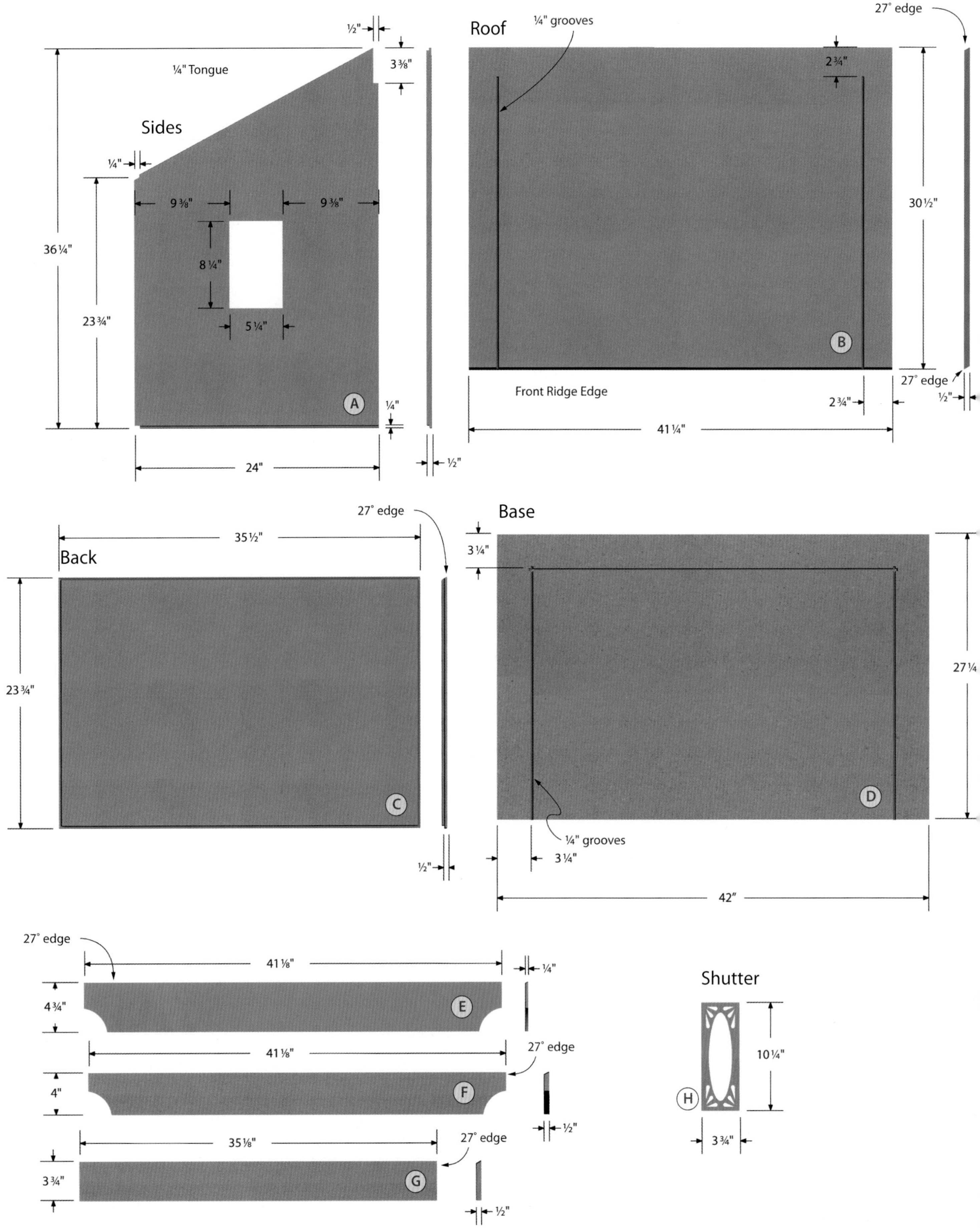
Sides
¼" Tongue
½"
3⅜"
¼"
36¼"
23¾"
9⅜"
9⅜"
8¼"
5¼"
A
¼"
24"
½"
Roof
¼" grooves
27° edge
2¾"
30½"
B
Front Ridge Edge
27° edge
2¾"
½"
41¼"
Back
35½"
27° edge
23¾"
C
½"
Base
3¼"
27¼
D
¼" grooves
3¼"
42"
27° edge
41⅛"
¼"
4¾"
E
41⅛"
27° edge
4"
F
½"
35⅛"
27° edge
3¾"
G
½"
Shutter
10¼"
H
3¾"

Full Size Templates

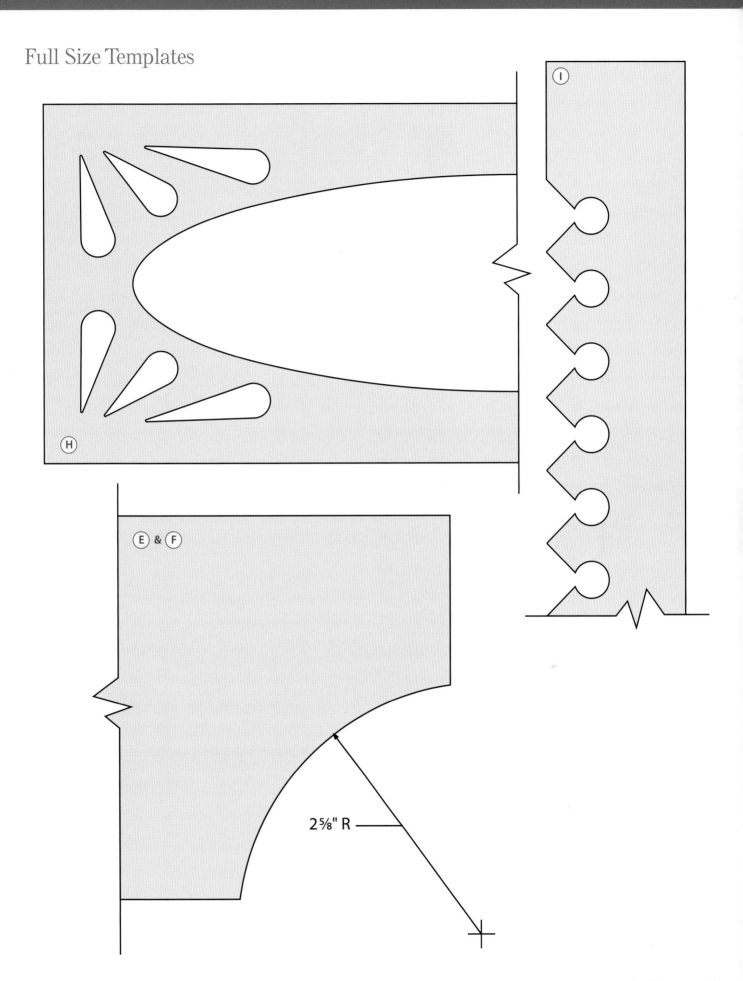

Ⓘ

Ⓗ

Ⓔ & Ⓕ

2⅝" R

Historical American Houses

Note the smoke hole and the pegs down the front of this Nez Perce tepee, photographed in 1900 near Spokane, Washington.

Pre 1900: Tepee

Some American Indian tribes lived in tepees made from animal hides, poles, and fiber woven into mats. This architectural style may be familiar to readers of the Kaya American Girl books.

Basic: To create a basic tepee, follow the instructions on page 33–34.

Detailed: To create a detailed tepee, follow the instructions on pages 33–34 with the following modifications: use leatherette material and real sticks instead of tan fabric and dowel rods. For a finishing touch, purchase a woven placemat or potholder from your local kitchen store and cut it down to size.

Note the protruding beams and adobe walls on this Spanish Colonial house.

1600–1850: Spanish Colonial

Many Americans who lived in the Southwest during the early 1800s built adobe Spanish Colonial houses. This architectural style may be familiar to readers of the Josefina American Girl books.

Basic: To create a basic Spanish Colonial dollhouse, you will need the following elements.

- Adobe (page 27)
- Stone spray paint (page 27), adobe
- Square windows (page 28)
- Flat roof (page 28)
- Protruding beams, simple (page 29)

Detailed: To create a detailed Spanish Colonial dollhouse, you will need the following elements.

- Stone spray paint (page 27) for adobe walls and earthen roof
- Protruding beams, detailed (page 32)

1700–1780: Georgian with brick

Many Georgian houses built in Northeastern cities before and during the Civil War were made of brick. This architectural style may be familiar to readers of the Addy American Girl books.

Basic: To create a basic brick Georgian dollhouse, you will need the following elements.

• Brick (page 27)

• Stone spray paint (page 27), brick

• Rectangular windows (page 14)

• Shingles (page 13)

• Gabled roof (page 28), side

• Sign (page 29), 12" x 2½", Ford's Dress Shop

• Shutters (page 14), green

Detailed: To create a detailed brick Georgian dollhouse, you will need the following elements.

• Gabled window (page 31)

• Picture window (page 31), rectangular

• Paneled shutters (page 32), green

Photo courtesy basykes.

Note the brick exterior, paneled shutters, and gabled windows of this Georgian home in Philadelphia, Pennsylvania.

1700–1780: Georgian with clapboard

Some early Americans living in Revolutionary-era Williamsburg, Virginia, had Georgian-style houses with clapboard. This architectural style may be familiar to readers of the Felicity American Girl books.

Basic: To create a basic colonial Georgian dollhouse, you will need the following elements.

• Brick (page 27), for bottom 4"

• Clapboard (page 13), white

• Stone spray paint (page 27), brick

• Rectangular windows (page 14)

• Shingles (page 13)

• Gabled roof (page 28), side

• Shutters (page 14), green

Detailed: To create a detailed colonial Georgian dollhouse, you will need the following elements.

• Gabled window (page 31)

• Corbels (page 32)

• Paneled shutters (page 32), green

Photo courtesy Bradley Jones.

The Raleigh Tavern, in Williamsburg, Virginia, is typical of a colonial Georgian house. Note the green paneled shutters, brick base with white clapboard above, and gabled windows.

Photo courtesy Brian Stansberry.

The William and Martha Jane Huskey Ogle Cabin, in Gatlinburg, Tennessee, was built in the 1800s. Note the stone base and corner formation.

Pre 1850–1890: Log House

Many settlers of the midlands during the pre-railroad era lived in log houses. This architectural style may be familiar to readers of the Kirsten American Girl books.

Basic: To create a basic log dollhouse, you will need the following elements.

- Square log (page 27)
- Rectangular windows (page 14)
- Shingles (page 13)
- Gabled roof (page 28), side

Detailed: To create a detailed log dollhouse, you will need the following elements.

- Stone (page 27), bottom 2"

Photo courtesy roanofthefour.

Photo courtesy Allan Ferguson.

Victorian and Italianate homes in San Francisco can be brightly painted and highly ornamented, with decorative molding, window hoods, and many other decorative elements.

1840–1885: Italianate

San Francisco, California, is well-known for its colorful and ornate Victorian and Italianate row homes. This architectural style may be familiar to readers of the Julie American Girl books.

Basic: To create a basic Italianate dollhouse, you will need the following elements.

- Clapboard (page 13), brightly colored
- Rectangular windows (page 14)
- Shingles (page 13)
- Flat roof (page 28)

Detailed: To create a detailed Italianate dollhouse, you will need the following elements.

- Arched window (page 30)
- Bay window (page 30), brightly painted, full height of house
- Corbels (page 32)
- Window hood (page 32)

1855–1885: Second Empire Victorian

Second Empire Victorian homes were popular on the East Coast during the 1900s. This architectural style may be familiar to readers of the Samantha American Girl books.

Basic: To create a basic Second Empire Victorian dollhouse, you will need the following elements.

- Clapboard (page 13), tan
- Rectangular windows (page 14)
- Shingles (page 13)
- Straight mansard roof (page 28–29)
- Shutters (page 14), green

Detailed: To create a detailed Second Empire Victorian dollhouse, you will need the following elements.

- Porch (page 30)
- Tower (page 30)
- Bay window (page 30)
- Gabled window (page 31)
- Picture window (page 31)
- Hexagonal shingles (page 31)
- Belt course (page 32), white
- Corbels (page 32)
- Cresting (page 32)
- Paneled shutters (page 32), green
- Window hood (page 32)

Photo courtesy BaRWoRlDv6.

Second Empire houses feature a mansard roof, towers, window hoods, and cresting on the roofline.

Photo courtesy james.thompson.

This house features both stone and clapboard, as well as a porch.

1880–1955: Colonial Revival

Colonial Revival homes are fairly common throughout the United States. This architectural style may be familiar to readers of the Kit American Girl books.

Basic: To create a basic Colonial Revival dollhouse, you will need the following elements.

- Clapboard (page 13), yellow, down to bottom of window, or second floor if building multiple modules
- Stone (page 27), gray, up to bottom of window, or first floor if building multiple modules
- Stone spray paint (page 27), gray
- Rectangular windows (page 14)
- Shingles (page 13)
- Gabled roof (page 28), side

Detailed: To create a detailed Colonial Revival dollhouse, you will need the following elements.

- Ivy (page 30)
- Porch (page 30)
- Bay window (page 30)
- Gabled window (page 31)
- Picture window (page 31), arched

Photo courtesy shadysidelantern.

Tudor Revival homes often have multiple and steep rooflines, arched doors, and an interesting blend of exterior cover.

1890–1940: Tudor Revival

Tudor Revival architecture was popular up to World War II. This architectural style may be familiar to readers of the Molly American Girl books.

Basic: To create a basic Tudor Revival dollhouse, you will need the following elements.

- Brick (page 27)
- Stone spray paint (page 27), red
- Rectangular windows (page 14)
- Shingles (page 13)
- Gabled roof (page 28), front

Detailed: To create a detailed Tudor Revival dollhouse, you will need the following elements.

- Brick (page 27), up to bottom of window, or first floor if building multiple modules
- Clapboard (page 13), white, down to bottom of window, or second floor if building multiple modules

Basic elements

Exterior choices

Adobe (Josefina): Use a flat piece of ⅛" Masonite for the walls. Paint the outsides with terra cotta stone spray paint (see "Stone spray paint", below).

Brick (Felicity, Addy, Molly): Use a router or Dremel with a ⅛" flat-bottom or standard flat bit to create a brick pattern on ⅛" Masonite by carving out the mortar areas. Spray the finished wall with red stone spray paint (see Stone spray paint, below). Paint the mortar lines white if desired.

Clapboard (Felicity, Samantha, Kit, Molly): See instructions on page 13.

Stone (Kit): Use a router or Dremel with a ⅛" flat-bottom or standard flat bit to create a stone pattern on ⅛" Masonite by carving out the mortar areas. Spray the finished wall with gray stone spray paint (see "Stone spray paint," below). Paint the mortar lines white if desired.

Square log (Kirsten): Cut 2" square stock to the length of the wall you'll be applying it to. If desired, notch the end of each log so the corners will create an authentic joint (see top photo on page 24). Paint three of the sides dark brown. Attach the "log" to the wall using adhesive and pin nails if necessary. Leave 1" of space between each log. Apply off-white caulk between the cracks to simulate mortar.

Stone spray paint (Felicity, Josefina, Addy, Kit, Molly): Stone spray paint applies as normal spray paint does. However, the stone paint adds additional texture, which gives the dried painted surface a stone look. You can cover the entire surface with the stone paint, or try applying regular acrylic paint to the surface with a brush and then coat lightly with stone spray for a speckled effect. Use red for brick, terra cotta for adobe, gray for stone, and brown for earthen roofs. Try products such as Rust-Oleum MultiColor Textured Spray Paint, American Accents Stone Creations, Krylon Make it Stone!, and others. You can also try drywall texturing spray—remember to sand the surface if you apply too much.

Adobe.

Brick.

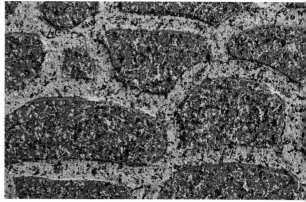
Stone.

Windows

Rectangular window (Felicity, Kirsten, Addy, Samantha, Kit, Molly, Julie): See instructions for Windows on page 14.

Square window (Josefina): Cut 7" x 7" square windows directly into the wall of the dollhouse using a jigsaw.

Roof choices

Plain shingles (Felicity, Kirsten, Addy, Samantha, Kit, Molly, Julie): See instructions for Shingles on page 13.

Flat roof (Josefina, Julie): To create a flat roof, simply cut the MDF to the same size as the width and length dimensions of the room, and cut the walls flat across the top. Lay the roof on top of the room and attach using screws and glue, or create a mortise-and-tenon joint.

Gabled roof (Felicity, Kirsten, Addy, Kit, Molly, Julie): The two types of gabled roof are the same, for dollhouse purposes. The only difference is the side-gabled roof is sloped toward the front and back of the house—meaning the door is under the slope—while the front-gabled roof slopes toward the sides—locating the door under the gable. Use the drawings on pages 15–20 to create the walls and roof for a gabled house.

Straight mansard roof (Samantha):

1. You will need different walls for a mansard roof than you would for a gabled roof. Create a front wall that is 24" x 36". Make two side walls that are 24" x 24". Cut an oversize ceiling that is 40" x 26".

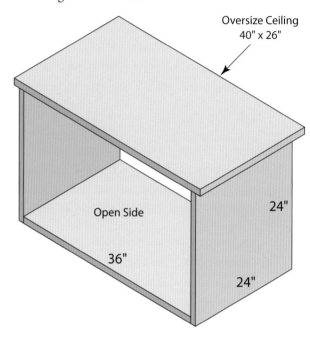

Oversize Ceiling
40" x 26"

Open Side

36"

24"

24"

2. Next, cut a piece of MDF to a rectangle that is smaller than the ceiling—this will be the top of the roof. Cut two 10"-high riser blocks that will fit under the top and attach them to the ceiling. Attach the top to the riser blocks.

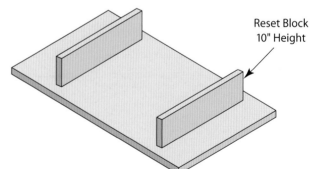

Reset Block
10" Height

3. Get some cardboard and hold it over the front of the roof between the top and ceiling pieces. Use a pencil to trace from the corner of the top to the corner of the bottom on both ends. Mark the top and bottom, and this will be your pattern.

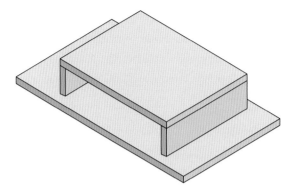

4. Cut a piece of ½" MDF to fit that pattern. Repeat on all sides.

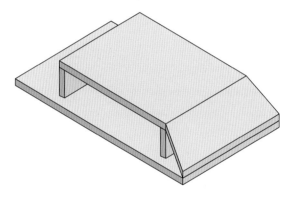

5. Use your fastener of choice to secure the roof pieces. Shingle as desired.

Here are more exact instructions for those of you who want them.

1. Create a front wall that is 24" x 36". Make two side walls that are 24" x 24". Cut a ceiling that is 42" x 30".

2. To create the pattern for the front piece of roof, make a 36" x 12" rectangle. Add triangles on the 12" ends of the rectangle with a 3" base and a 12⅜" hypotenuse.

3. To create the pattern for the two sides, make a 24" x 12" rectangle and add a triangle on one of the 12" sides that has a 3" base and a 12⅜" hypotenuse.

4. To cut the pieces, set your miter box at 45° with a tilt of 70°.

5. Assemble—glue if desired. Shingle as desired.

Details

Plain shutters (Felicity, Addy, Samantha): See instructions on page 14.

Protruding beam, simple (Josefina): Cut 1½" square stock or 1½" diameter dowels into 3"-long pieces. Attach two of the "beams" to the side walls near the roof so they protrude outward, parallel with the ground. In real Spanish Colonial homes, these protruding beams support the roof.

Sign (Addy): Cut ¼"-thick wood into the sign shape desired. Paint with a light color. To create letters, paint them on with a darker color by hand or with a stencil, or create them on your computer and print on sticky label to attach to the sign.

Detailed elements

Exterior choices

Ivy (Kit): Use paint or a rub-on transfer decal to put ivy on the walls. You could also apply the decal to a piece of MDF and use the scroll saw to cut around it, giving you a long vine of ivy that can be glued or nailed where desired. Another option is buying artificial ivy from a craft store.

Porch (Samantha, Kit): If you wish to make a porch, you can make the baseboard of the dollhouse large in the direction where the porch will be or build the porch on its own base so it is movable. Use ½" square wood for posts and make a gabled roof to fit.

Tower (Samantha): You will need three pieces of MDF cut to 36" x 6" or one solid piece of wood with those dimensions. Create a smaller version of the mansard roof directions on pages 28–29 and attach it to the top of the tower. Nail the tower to the dollhouse where desired.

Windows

Arched window (Samantha, Kit, Molly, Julie): Follow the directions for Rectangular Windows (page 14). Instead of a straight top, use a compass to make an arch with the middle as the highest point at 4".

Bay window (Samantha, Kit, Julie): You will need a 2 x 6. Cut off two wedges at 45°. Use the scroll saw to cut out window openings and trim the excess wood inside with hand tools.

Photo courtesy AlexPears

Ivy.

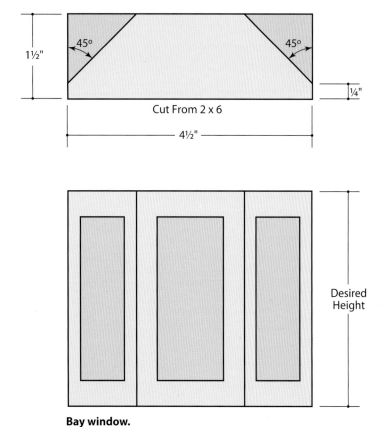

Bay window.

Gabled window (Felicity, Addy, Samantha, Kit): Glue together a wood block to desired dimensions. Cut off two wedges using a table saw. Cut to length and slope angle using a miter saw. Cut two panels of ½" MDF as roof cover. Make window trim for a fake window. Finally, cover with shingles and siding of choice. (See drawings on this page).

Picture window (Addy, Kit, Samantha): Follow directions for Rectangular Windows (page 14) or Arched Window (opposite page). Modify the window measurements as follows: Rectangular picture windows should have the exterior rectangle at 9" x 12" and the interior rectangle at 7" x 10". Arched picture windows should also be 9" x 12", with the center of the arch at 3".

Roof choices

Hexagonal shingles (Samantha): Follow the instructions for making Shingles (page 13). Cut the corners off one end of each shingle so there is a flat side between them. Also, sheets of copper embossed with a hexagonal shingle pattern are available, such as part number 96949 from Wildwood Designs, 800-470-9090, *www.wildwooddesigns.com.*

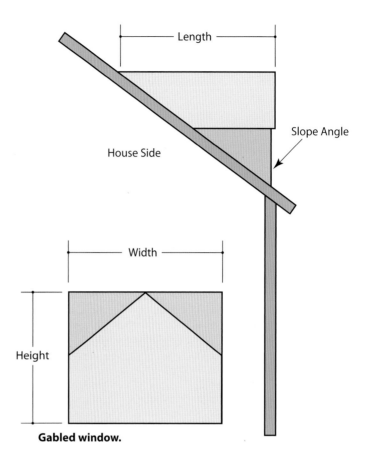

Gabled window.

Details

Belt course (Samantha): Use desired paint color to paint a 1½"-thick line across the house.

Cresting (Samantha): Use ⅛" dowels to make a row of posts along the top of the roofline. Another option is to use a scroll saw to cut a fancy line of running trim and attach it to the roof.

Corbels (Felicity, Samantha, Julie): Making a corbel for a dollhouse is like making a sandwich. You will have a ½"-thick piece of plain wood in the middle with a scroll-sawn ⅛"-thick piece on either side. Stack cut the two thin pieces as desired, or use the pattern given. Then cut a ½"-thick piece of wood, profile only. Glue the three pieces together and attach to house under the roofline. You could also carve a design on the corbels if desired.

Paneled shutters (Felicity, Addy, Samantha): Follow directions for Shutters (page 14). Prior to painting, use a router to cut panels onto the shutters. You could also create shutters from two layers of wood: the top layer has holes cut out, and the under layer is plain.

Protruding beam, detailed (Josefina): Cut 1½" square holes through the side walls at the top so a 42"-long 1½" square piece of wood can sit in the holes and run straight through under the roof. If using 1½" dowels, drill holes through the walls.

Window hood (Samantha, Julie): Cut a design into a ⅛"-thick piece of wood that is 1" wider than and a third as tall as the window you're creating the hood for. Glue the ⅛" piece onto a ½"-thick piece of the same length and width. Cut the glued piece into a shape that fits around the top of the window frame.

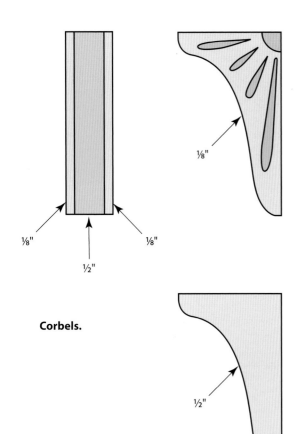

Corbels.

Plans for Kaya's tepee

1. Cut a half-circle from the fabric that is 64" on its long edge, and 32" across. An easy way to do this is to measure 32" across the top to find the middle, and then keeping the ruler on the middle point, move the ruler around that point and mark the 32" point multiple times.

2. Cut a half arch on the end of each long edge so that when the two edges come together, a doorway is created. The doorway should be about 8" wide at the bottom, and at least as tall. Also cut the slits for the pegs.

3. Use a clove hitch knot to tie the tips of three dowels into a tripod, as shown.

4. Set up the tripod and place the other three dowels. Tie them on.

5. Place the fabric around the poles. There should be a slight hole at the top to accommodate the poles.

6. Insert the pegs through the slits. If needed, stitch between the top of the doorway and the top of the tepee.

Tools and Materials

- 36" (914mm)-long ¼" (6mm) dowels, 6 (tepee poles)
- Toothpicks, 5 (pegs to close front)
- 32" x 64" (813mm x 1626mm) rectangle of fabric of choice (leatherette if you want to be more accurate)
- Scissors

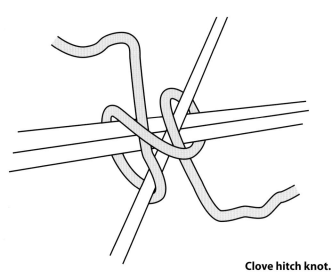

Clove hitch knot.

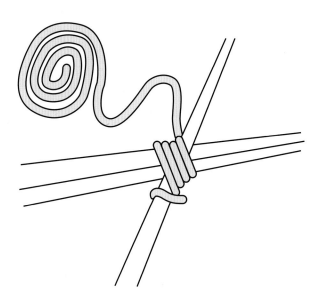

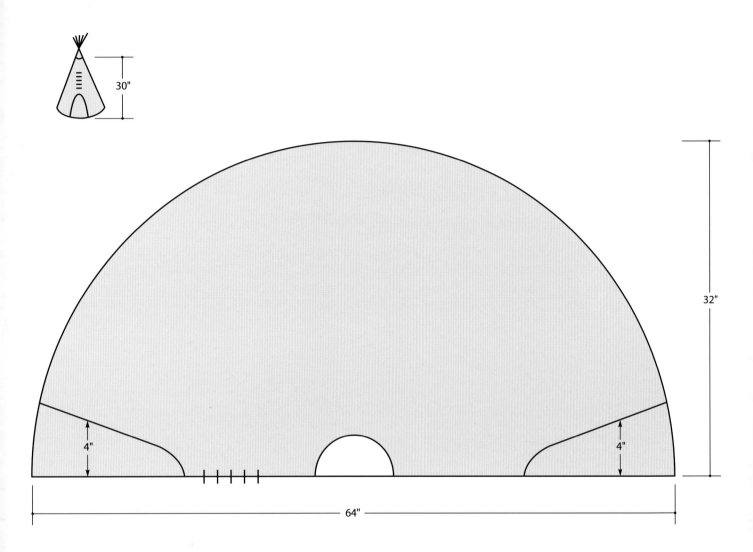

30"

32"

4"

4"

64"

Chairs

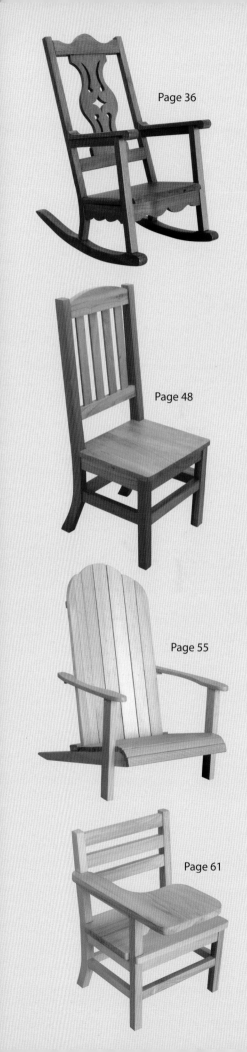

Page 36

Page 48

Page 55

Page 61

First and foremost, a doll should have a chair. Whether the doll is an heirloom placed on a shelf for safekeeping or a treasured companion of a small child, a chair is a necessity. Chairs allow heirloom dolls to be displayed prominently and encourage children to become involved in creative play with their small counterparts.

Seating arrangements for dolls are as unique and varied as they are for the dolls' human handlers. With a little bit of effort, almost any adult-sized chair can be duplicated on a smaller scale for an 18" doll. Here in this chapter you will find four varieties of chairs: a rocking chair, a dining chair, an Adirondack chair, and an old-fashioned chair desk.

When making chairs, give intensive effort to accurately cutting the individual pieces to the dimensions indicated on the drawings. Many of the chair pieces are joined together with mortise and tenon joints. Accurately cut and fitted pieces are required for a strong joint because the glue is the only thing holding the assembly together. Mortise and tenon joints are precisely made using a mortising tool found in home centers. An inexpensive mortising attachment for a drill press was used in making the chairs in this book.

Rocking Chair

Materials List

Item	Width	Length	Thickness	Quantity	Material	Location
Arm	¾" (19mm)	5¾" (146mm)	¾" (19mm)	2	Walnut	Page 42
Arm Support	½" (13mm)	5⅛" (130mm)	½" (13mm)	2	Walnut	Page 40
Back	3" (76mm)	7¼" (184mm)	⅜" (10mm)	1	Walnut	Page 43
Back Stretcher	¾" (19mm)	6" (152mm)	½" (13mm)	1	Walnut	Page 41
Front Stretcher	1" (25mm)	6" (152mm)	⅜" (10mm)	2	Walnut	Page 41
Left Front Leg	½" (13mm)	7" (178mm)	½" (13mm)	1	Walnut	Page 40
Left Leg	2¼" (57mm)	12⅜" (314mm)	½" (13mm)	1	Walnut	Page 45
Right Front Leg	½" (13mm)	7" (178mm)	½" (13mm)	1	Walnut	Page 40
Right Leg	2¼" (57mm)	12⅜" (314mm)	½" (13mm)	1	Walnut	Page 44
Rocker	2¾" (70mm)	11½" (292mm)	¾" (19mm)	2	Walnut	Page 46
Seat	5" (127mm)	6⅜" (162mm)	⅜" (10mm)	1	Walnut	Page 47
Side Stretcher	1" (25mm)	4⅜" (111mm)	⅜" (10mm)	2	Walnut	Page 42
Splat	1½" (38mm)	6" (152mm)	½" (13mm)	1	Walnut	Page 43

Making the Legs

1. Select hardwood materials of the proper thickness for each chair part.

2. Cut the Left Front Leg and the Right Front Leg to the sizes specified on the drawings.

3. Photocopy the drawings for the Left Leg and the Right Leg. Use temporary adhesive to attach the photocopy to the wood selected for these pieces. Ensure that the straight edge of the photocopy is aligned with the edge of the board. Cut the angle cuts and leave the remainder of the board attached to the Left Leg and the Right Leg, as shown on the drawing.

4. Lay out the locations of the mortises specified on the drawings for the Left Front Leg, the Left Leg, the Right Front Leg and the Right Leg.

5. Use a ¼" mortise drill and cut all mortises ⅜" deep and to the length specified on the drawings.

> **Technical Note:**
> The Legs must remain attached to the wood pieces until after the mortises have been cut in the Leg pieces.

Making the Back

6. Photocopy the pattern for the Splat. Use temporary adhesive to attach the photocopy to the wood selected for the Splat.

7. Cut the materials to make the Splat and the Back Stretcher.

8. Lay out the locations of the mortises on the edge of these pieces as specified on the drawings.

9. Use a ¼" mortise drill and cut the mortises ⅜" deep and to the length specified on the drawings.

10. Lay out and cut the tenons on both ends of these pieces to the dimensions specified on the drawings.

11. Cut the decorative top profile on the Splat, following the lines on the photocopy.

12. Cut a piece of wood for the Back to the size specified on the drawing.

13. Photocopy the drawing for the Back. Use temporary adhesive to attach the photocopy to the wood selected for the Back.

14. Lay out and cut the tenons on both ends of these pieces to the dimensions specified on the drawing.

15. Drill pilot holes for the blade and use a scroll saw to cut the decorative profile for the Back.

16. Dry fit the Back with the Splat and the Back Stretcher. Dry fit the Back Assembly with the Left Leg and the Right Leg.

17. Apply glue to the tenons on the Back and to the mortises in the Splat and in the Back Stretcher. Clamp the Back Assembly, ensuring the assembly is square.

Making the Stretchers

18. Cut the Arm Supports, the Side Stretchers and the Front Stretchers to the sizes specified on the drawings.

19. Lay out and cut the tenons on both ends of these pieces to the dimensions specified on the drawings.

20. Photocopy the pattern for the Side Stretcher and the Front Stretcher pieces. Use temporary adhesive to attach the photocopy to these pieces.

21. Cut the decorative profile on the bottom edges of the Side Stretchers and the Front Stretcher.

22. Dry assemble all of the Stretcher pieces with the Legs made above. Ensure all of the tenons fit the mortises in the legs.

Assembling the Chair

23. Apply glue to the tenons on the Front Stretcher and to the mortises in the Left Front Leg and the Right Front Leg and clamp. Ensure that the assembly is square and that the unused mortises on the Front Legs are oriented in the same direction.

24. Apply glue to the tenons on the Splat, the Back Stretcher and the Front Stretcher. Apply glue to the mortises in the Left Leg and the Right Leg.

25. Clamp the Back Leg Assembly together, ensuring the assembly is square.

26. Apply glue to the tenons on the Side Stretchers, the Arm Supports and the mortises in the Leg Assemblies. Clamp the Chair Assembly together, ensuring that the assembly is square.

27. Photocopy the pattern for the Seat. Use temporary adhesive to attach the photocopy.

28. Cut the Seat to the size specified on the drawing and cut the notches in the Seat for the Legs.

29. Dry fit the Seat with the Chair Assembly.

30. Use a file and a sanding block to round over the front edge of the Seat, as shown on the drawing.

31. Apply glue to the top edge of the Stretchers and clamp the Seat to the Chair Assembly.

32. Photocopy the drawing for the Arm pieces. Use temporary adhesive to attach the photocopy to the wood selected for the Arms.

33. Cut the decorative profile for the Arms using a scroll saw.

34. Glue and clamp the Arms to the Arm Supports.

Making the Rockers

35. Photocopy the drawing for the Rockers. Use temporary adhesive to attach the photocopy to the wood selected for the Rockers. Ensure the straight edge of the photocopy is aligned with the edge of the wood piece.

36. Cut the decorative profile on the topside of the Rockers.

37. Cut the 22° angle cut and leave the Rockers attached to the remainder of the boards, as shown on the drawing.

38. Lay out the locations of the mortises shown on the drawing to match the tenons on the assembled chair.

39. Use a ¼" mortise drill and cut the mortises ⅜" deep and to the length specified on the drawing.

40. Dry fit the assembled rocking chair with the Rockers.

41. Cut the decorative profile on the bottom side of the Rockers.

42. Glue and clamp the Rockers to the Chair Assembly.

Finishing

43. Sand the assembled rocking chair and apply a finish.

Technical Note:
The Rockers must remain attached to the wood pieces until after the mortises have been cut.

Technical Note:
The mortise locations shown on the Rocker drawing indicate the proper location for the mortises if all of the chair's components are made precisely as specified on the drawings. Any variation in component sizes could result in a mismatched fit with the Rockers. It is best to lay the assembled rocking chair along-side the Rockers to compare the tenons on the chair with the mortise locations on the photocopy. Re-mark the mortise locations as needed to fit with the assembled chair.

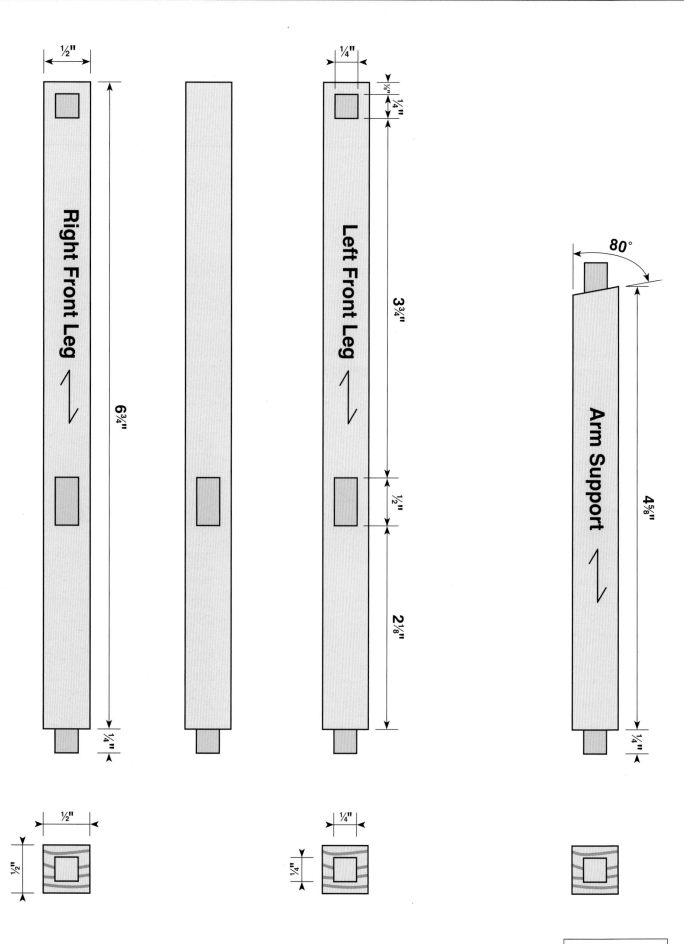

Right Front Leg ↘

½"

6¾"

¼"

Left Front Leg ↘

¼"

⅛"

¼"

3¾"

½"

2⅛"

¼"

Arm Support ↘

80°

4⅝"

¼"

½"

½"

¼"

¼"

Shown actual size.

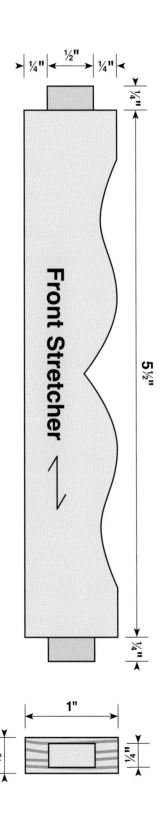

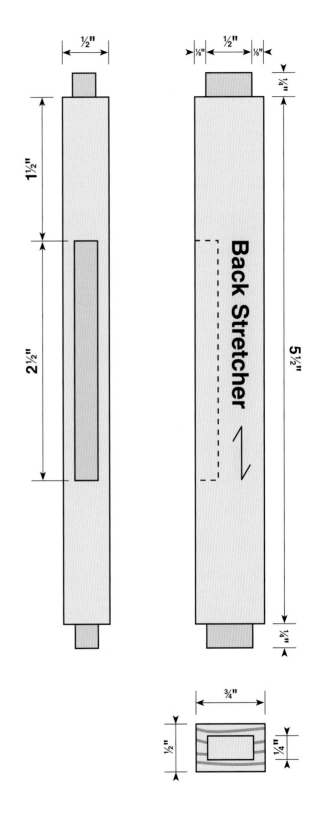

Shown actual size.

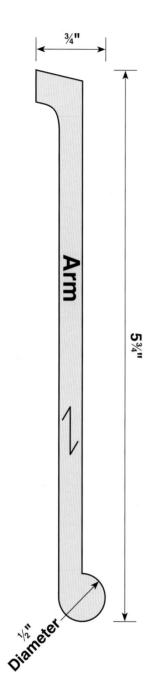

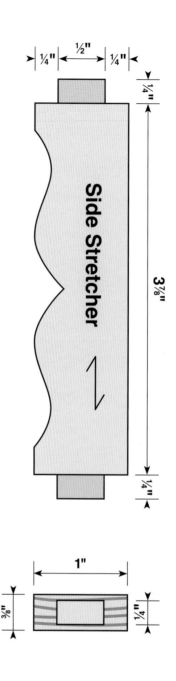

Side Stretcher

3⁷⁄₈"

¼" ½" ¼"

¼"

¼"

1"

3⁄₈"

¼"

Arm

5¾"

½" Diameter

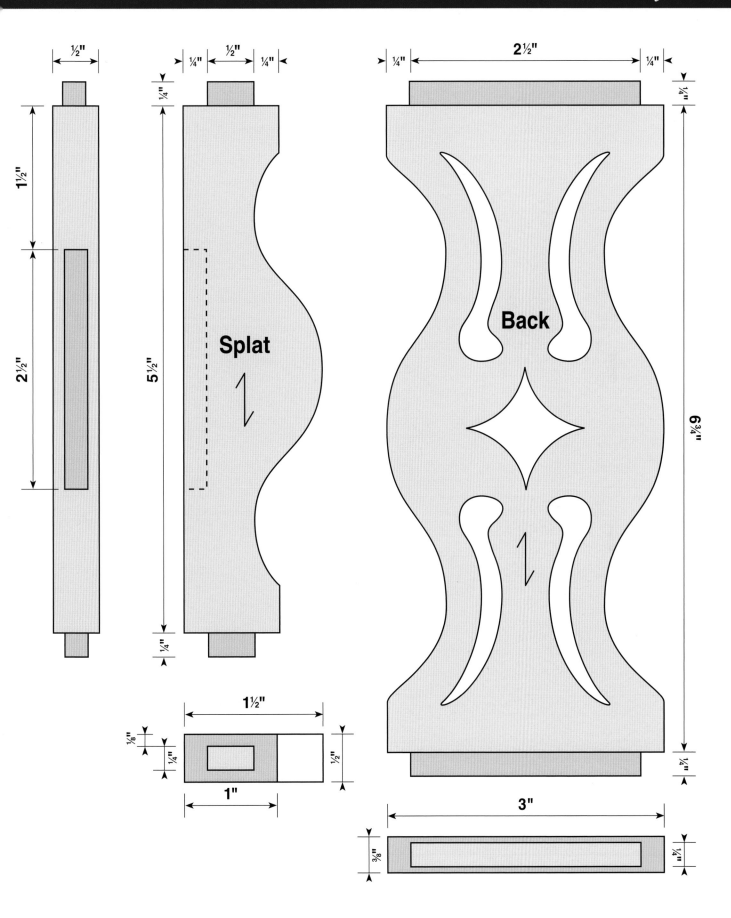

Splat

Back

Shown actual size.

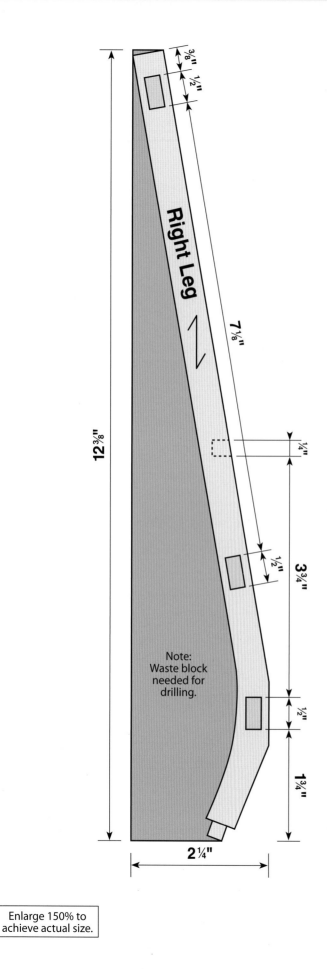

Right Leg

3/8"

1/2"

7 1/8"

12 3/8"

1/4"

1/2"

3 3/4"

Note:
Waste block
needed for
drilling.

1/2"

1 3/4"

2 1/4"

Enlarge 150% to
achieve actual size.

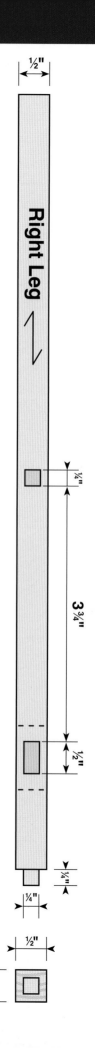

1/2"

Right Leg

1/4"

3 3/4"

1/2"

1/4"

1/4"

1/2"

1/2"

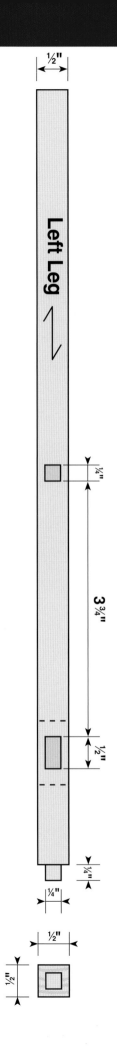

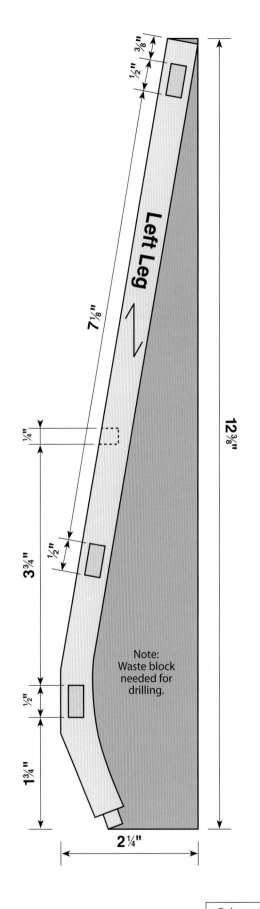

½"

Left Leg

¼"

3¾"

½"

¼"

¼"

½"

½"

3/8"

½"

Left Leg

7⅛"

¼"

12⅜"

3¾"

½"

Note:
Waste block
needed for
drilling.

½"

1¾"

2¼"

Enlarge 150% to
achieve actual size.

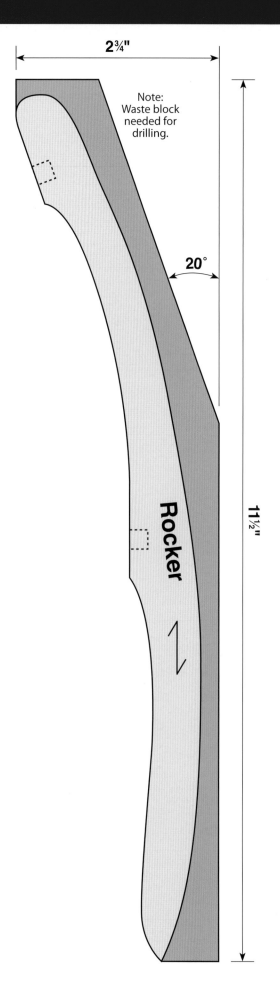

2¾"

Note:
Waste block
needed for
drilling.

20°

Rocker

11½"

Enlarge 125% to
achieve actual size.

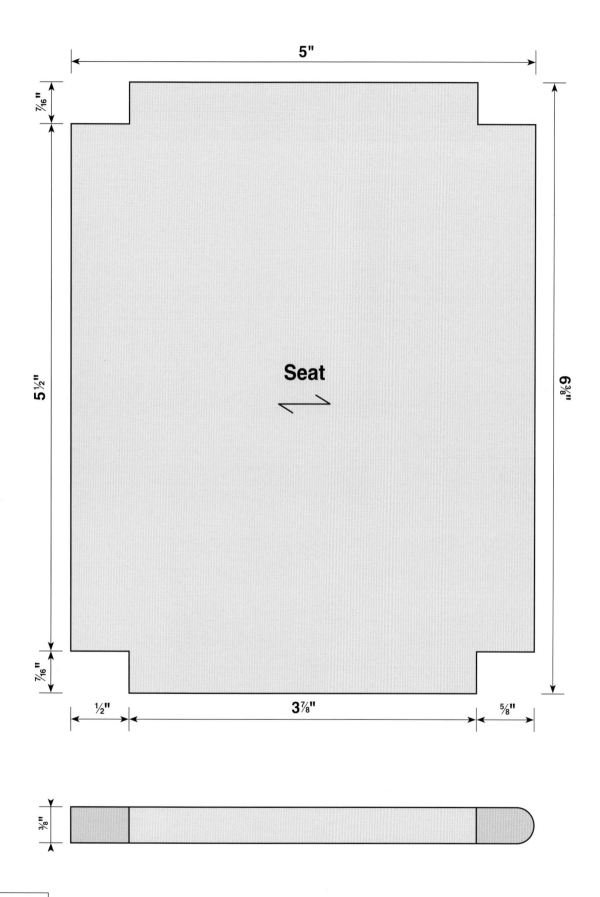

5"

7/16"

5½"

6⅜"

Seat

7/16"

½"

3⅞"

⅝"

⅜"

Shown actual size.

Dining Chair

Materials List

Item	Width	Length	Thickness	Quantity	Material	Location
Back Slat	⅝" (16mm)	4" (102mm)	⅛" (3mm)	4	Cherry	Page 52
Back Stretcher	¾" (19mm)	5¼" (133mm)	⅜" (10mm)	1	Cherry	Page 51
Front Leg	½" (13mm)	4⅜" (111mm)	½" (13mm)	2	Cherry	Page 53
Left Leg	2" (51mm)	11½" (292mm)	½" (13mm)	1	Cherry	Page 54
Lower Side Stretcher	⅝" (16mm)	4½" (114mm)	⅜" (10mm)	2	Cherry	Page 53
Lower Stretcher	⅝" (16mm)	5¼" (133mm)	⅜" (10mm)	2	Cherry	Page 51
Right Leg	2" (51mm)	11½" (292mm)	½" (13mm)	1	Cherry	Page 54
Seat	5⅛" (13cm)	5⅞" (149mm)	⅜" (10mm)	1	Cherry	Page 52
Splat	1¼" (32mm)	5¼" (133mm)	⅜" (10mm)	1	Cherry	Page 51
Upper Side Stretcher	¾" (19mm)	4½" (114mm)	⅜" (10mm)	2	Cherry	Page 53
Upper Stretcher	¾" (19mm)	5¼" (133mm)	⅜" (10mm)	2	Cherry	Page 51

Making the Legs

1. Select hardwood materials of the proper thickness for each chair part.

2. Cut the Front Legs to the size specified on the drawing.

3. Photocopy the drawings for the Left Leg and the Right Leg pieces. Use temporary adhesive to attach the photocopy to the wood. Ensure the straight edge of the photocopy is aligned with the edge of the wood piece. Cut the angle cuts and leave the remainder of the boards attached to the Legs as shown on the drawings.

Technical Note:
The Legs must remain attached to the wood pieces until after the mortises have been cut in the Leg pieces.

Making the Splat and the Stretchers

4. Cut the materials to make the Splat and the Back Stretcher.

The Splat and the Back

5. Cut a ⅛" x ⅛" dado groove on the edges of the boards for the Splat and the Back Stretcher pieces.

6. Lay out and cut the tenons on both ends of these pieces to the dimensions specified on the drawings.

7. Photocopy the pattern for the Splat. Use temporary adhesive to attach the photocopied pattern; then cut the rounded top profile on the Splat.

8. Cut the Upper and Lower Stretchers and the Upper and Lower Side Stretchers to the sizes specified.

9. Lay out and cut the tenons on both ends of these pieces to the dimensions specified on the drawings.

10. Cut the Back Slats to the size specified on the drawing.

Technical Note:
Stretcher pieces have a dado groove cut in the edge. These pieces are too small to handle safely when cutting the dado. Cut the dado in an oversized board before cutting the pieces to their final widths and lengths. This improves the safety of the dado operation.

11. Cut ten pieces of wood ⅛" x ⅛" and ½" long. These will need to be trimmed to final length at assembly. Glue these into the dado groove in the Splat and the Back Stretcher. These pieces act as spacers and fill in the dado groove between the Back Slats.

12. Glue and clamp these spacers to the Splat and the Back Stretcher.

Assembling the Chair

13. Dry assemble all of the Stretcher pieces with the Legs made above. Be sure the tenons fit the mortises in the Legs.

14. Apply glue to the tenons on the Upper Stretchers and the Lower Stretchers and to the mortises in the two Front Legs. Clamp.

15. Ensure the assembly is square and the unused mortises on the Front Legs are oriented in the same direction.

16. Apply glue to the tenons on the Splat, the Back Stretcher and the Upper and Lower Stretchers. Apply glue to the mating mortises in the Left Leg and the Right Leg. Clamp the Back Leg Assembly together, ensuring that the assembly is square.

17. Apply glue to the tenons on the Upper and Lower Side Stretchers and the mortises in the Leg Assemblies. Clamp the Chair Assembly together, ensuring the assembly is square.

18. Cut the Seat to the size specified on the drawing. Cut the notches in the Seat for the Left and Right Legs. Dry fit the Seat with the Chair Assembly.

19. Apply glue to the top edge of the Stretchers and clamp the Seat to the Chair Assembly.

Finishing

20. Sand the chair and apply a finish.

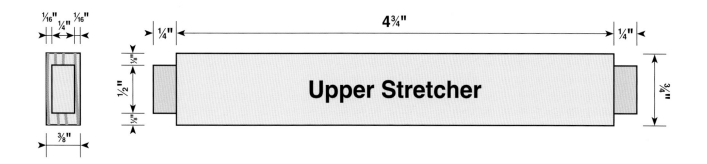

Upper Stretcher

Lower Stretcher

Back Stretcher

Shown actual size.

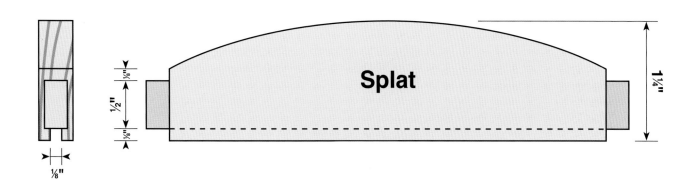

Splat

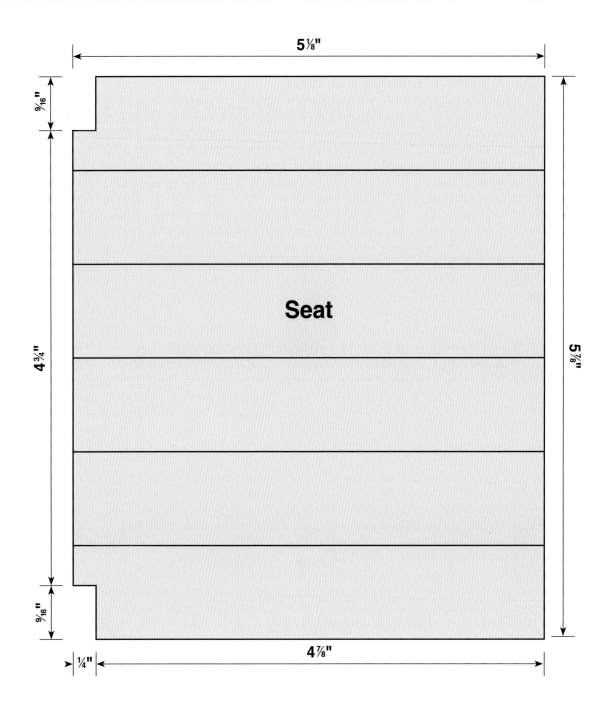

5⅛"

9/16"

4¾"

5⅞"

Seat

9/16"

¼"

4⅞"

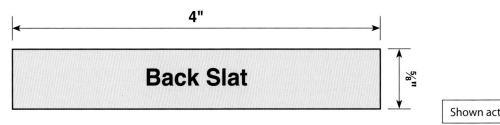

4"

Back Slat

5/8"

Shown actual size.

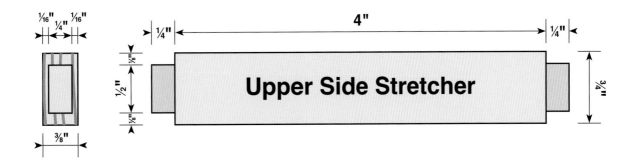

Upper Side Stretcher

Lower Side Stretcher

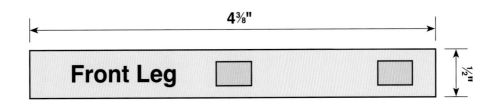

Front Leg

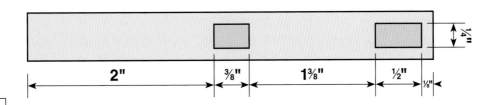

Shown actual size.

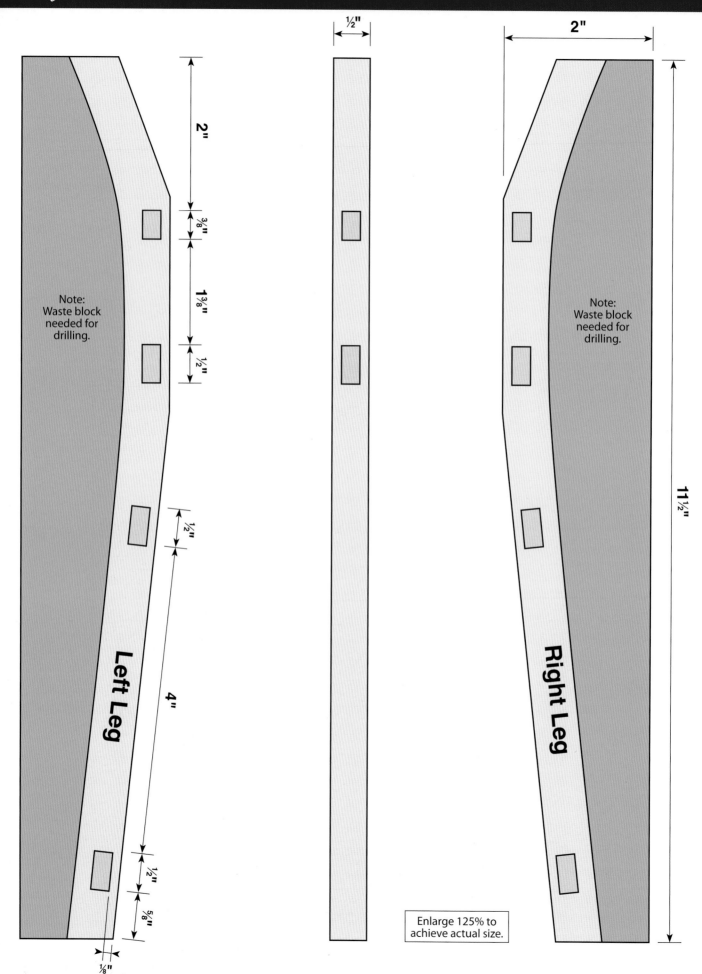

½"

2"

2"

3⁄8"

1 3⁄8"

½"

Note:
Waste block
needed for
drilling.

Note:
Waste block
needed for
drilling.

11½"

½"

4"

Left Leg

Right Leg

½"

5⁄8"

Enlarge 125% to
achieve actual size.

⅛"

½"

Adirondack Chair

Materials List

Item	Width	Length	Thickness	Quantity	Material	Location
Arm	1⅛" (29mm)	7⅞" (20cm)	¼" (6mm)	2	Poplar	Page 60
Assembly Template	1¾" (44mm)	7¾" (197mm)	⅜" (10mm)	1	Poplar	Page 59
Back	6" (152mm)	11" (279mm)	¼" (6mm)	1	Poplar	Page 58
Back Bow	1¾" (44mm)	6⅞" (175mm)	⅜" (10mm)	3	Poplar	Page 60
Front Leg	¾" (19mm)	5¾" (146mm)	⅜" (10mm)	2	Poplar	No drawing
Leg	⅞" (22mm)	11¼" (285mm)	⅜" (10mm)	2	Poplar	Page 59
Rear Slat	1¾" (44mm)	6⅞" (175mm)	¼" (6mm)	1	Poplar	Page 60
Seat Slat	½" (13mm)	6⅞" (175mm)	¼" (6mm)	10	Poplar	Page 60

Making the Chair

1. Select wood of the proper thickness for each chair part. Select wood with a fine grain in scale with the furniture being built.

2. Photocopy the drawing for the Legs. Use temporary adhesive to attach the photocopy to the wood selected for the Legs and cut out the two Legs.

3. Cut the Front Legs and the Seat Slats to the sizes specified on the drawings.

4. Photocopy the drawings for the Rear Slat, the Arm and the Back Bow pieces. Use temporary adhesive to attach these photocopies to the wood. Cut out each piece.

5. Photocopy the drawing for the Back. Use temporary adhesive to attach the photocopy to the wood selected for the Back. Then cut the profile for the Back.

6. Cut the Back into individual slats by cutting on the slat lines as indicated on the drawing.

7. Start at the front of the Legs and glue and clamp the Seat Slats to the two Legs.

8. Ensure the Seat Slats are flush with the sides of the Legs and that the assembly is square.

9. Glue and clamp the Rear Slat to the assembly.

Technical Note:
Lay out the Back pieces in the order they were cut. Take the outer two pieces from the set and reverse sides. Do the same with the pair on both sides of the centerpiece. Mixing these pieces changes the grain pattern and makes the assembly look like it was made from separate pieces of wood.

10. Glue and clamp the Front Legs to each side of the assembly. The Front Legs will be set back from the front end of the assembly by 1½" and extend 1¾" below the assembly. Ensure the Front Legs are square with the workbench top when they are placed in the normal use position.

11. Glue and clamp one of the Back Bow cutouts to the bottom edges of the Back pieces. Ensure these pieces are square to the Back Bow.

12. Glue and clamp the Back Assembly into position with the Chair Leg Assembly.

13. Place the Chair Assembly on the workbench top with the chair in the upright position.

14. Clamp the Arms and the center Back Bow to the Chair Assembly. Ensure the Arms will be 5¾" up the bench top. Mark the location where the center Back Bow should be glued to the Back Assembly.

15. Glue and clamp the center Back Bow to the Back Assembly.

16. Glue and clamp the top Back Bow to the Back Assembly near the top of the assembly.

17. Glue and clamp the Arms to the center Back Bow and the Front Legs. Small finish brad nails could be used to strengthen the connection of the Arms to the Front Legs.

18. Sand the chair and apply a finish.

Technical Note:
Adding the Front Legs to the assembly above can be easier if an Assembly Template is used. Make the Template by cutting a triangle from scrap wood. The Template will help align the Front Legs to the assembly.

Technical Note:
The angle of the Back Bow (when clamped to the Back Assembly) and the angle of the Arms (when attached to the Front Legs) do not fit together correctly. The ends of this Back Bow piece will need a small angle cut where the Arms attach. These small angle cuts are not shown on the drawing.

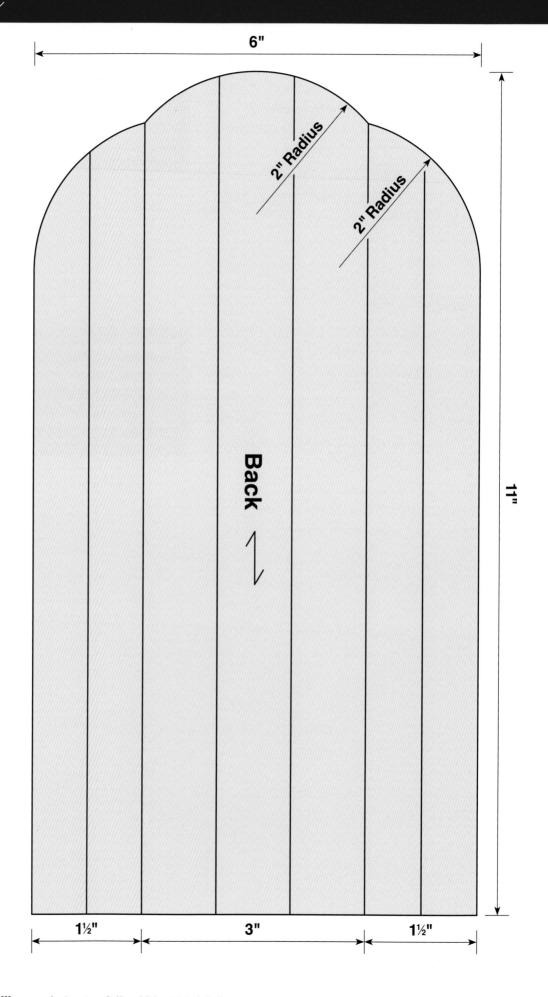

6"

11"

2" Radius

2" Radius

Back

1½"

3"

1½"

Enlarge 125% to achieve actual size.

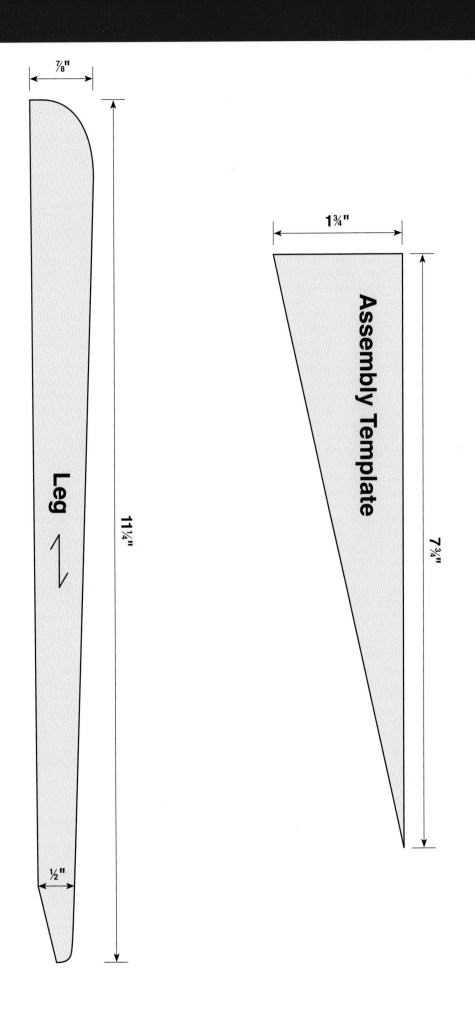

7/8"

1¾"

Assembly Template

Leg

11¼"

7¾"

½"

Enlarge 125% to achieve actual size.

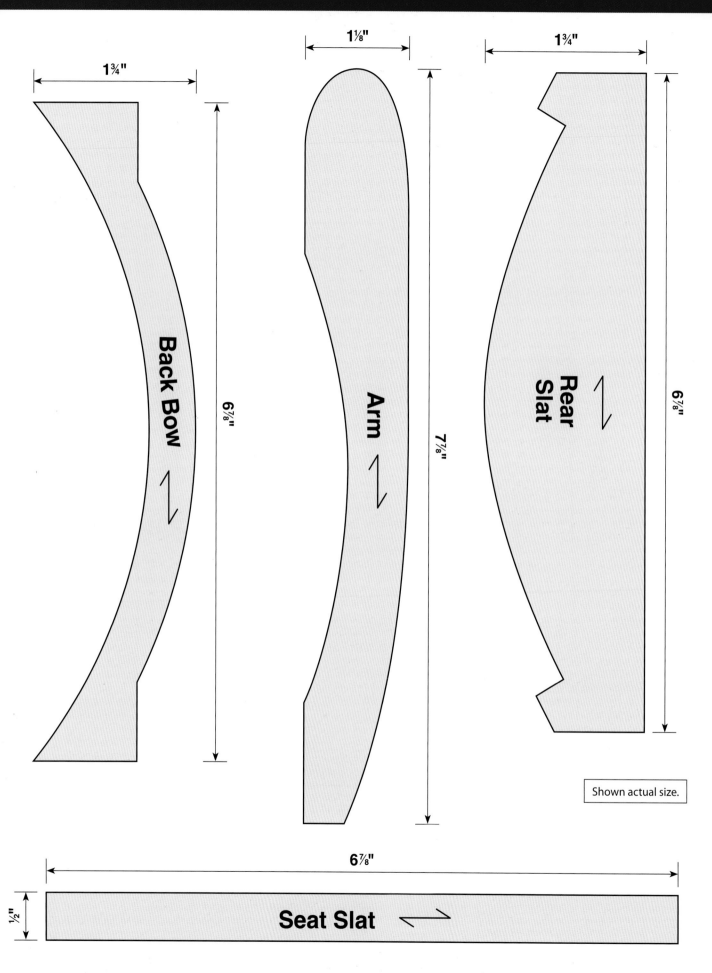

1¾"

1⅛"

1¾"

Back Bow

6⅞"

Arm

7⅞"

Rear Slat

6⅞"

Shown actual size.

6⅞"

½"

Seat Slat

Chair Desk

Materials List

Item	Width	Length	Thickness	Quantity	Material	Location
Arm Leg	½" (13mm)	7" (178mm)	½" (13mm)	1	Birch	Page 65
Arm Support	½" (13mm)	4¹³⁄₁₆" (122mm)	½" (13mm)	1	Birch	Page 67
Bottom Side Stretcher	½" (13mm)	4½" (114mm)	⅜" (10mm)	2	Birch	Page 64
Desk Top	4" (102mm)	8" (203mm)	⅜" (10mm)	1	Birch	Page 67
Front Leg	½" (13mm)	4⅛" (105mm)	½" (13mm)	1	Birch	Page 65
Left Leg	1½" (38mm)	9¾" (248mm)	½" (13mm)	1	Birch	Page 66
Lower Stretcher	½" (13mm)	5¾" (146mm)	⅜" (10mm)	2	Birch	Page 64
Right Leg	1½" (38mm)	9¾" (248mm)	½" (13mm)	1	Birch	Page 66
Seat	5⅜" (137mm)	6⅝" (168mm)	⅜" (10mm)	1	Birch	Page 68
Top Side Stretcher	¾" (19mm)	4½" (114mm)	⅜" (10mm)	2	Birch	Page 64
Top Support	1¾" (45mm)	1½" (38mm)	½" (13mm)	1	Birch	Page 67
Upper Stretcher & Slat	¾" (19mm)	5¾" (146mm)	⅜" (10mm)	5	Birch	Page 64

Making the Legs

1. Select hardwood materials of the proper thickness for each chair part.

2. Cut the Arm Leg and the Front Leg to the sizes specified on the drawings.

3. Photocopy the drawings for the Left Leg and the Right Leg pieces. Use temporary adhesive to attach the photocopy to the wood. Ensure the straight edge of the photocopy is aligned with the edge of the wood piece. Cut the angle cuts and leave the remainder of the boards attached to the Legs, as shown on the drawing.

4. Lay out the locations of the mortises specified on the drawings for the Arm Leg, the Front Leg, the Left Leg and the Right Leg. Note: The mortise for the Arm Support is only cut in the Left Leg.

5. Use a ¼" mortise drill and cut all mortises ⅜" deep and to the lengths specified on the drawings.

Technical Note:
The Legs must remain attached to the wood pieces until after the mortises have been cut in the Leg pieces.

Making the Chair Assembly

6. Cut the materials to the sizes specified on the drawings to make the Arm Support, the Top Side Stretcher, the Bottom Side Stretcher, the Lower Stretcher, the Upper Stretcher, and the Slat pieces.

7. Lay out and cut the tenons on both ends of these pieces to the dimensions specified on the drawings.

8. Dry assemble all the Stretcher pieces with the Legs made above. Ensure all tenons fit the mortises in the Legs.

9. Apply glue to the tenons on one Upper Stretcher & Slat and one Lower Stretcher. Apply glue to the mortises in the Arm Leg and the Front Leg. Ensure the assembly is square and the unused mortises on the Arm Leg and the Front Leg are oriented in the same direction.

10. Apply glue to the tenons on the four remaining Upper Stretcher & Slat pieces and one Lower Stretcher. Apply glue to the mortises in the Left and the Right Legs. Clamp the Back Leg Assembly together, ensuring the assembly is square.

11. Apply glue to the tenons on the two Top Side Stretchers, the two Bottom Side Stretchers, the Arm Support, and the mortises in the Leg Assemblies. Clamp the Chair Assembly together, ensuring the assembly is square.

Making the Seat

12. Photocopy the drawing for the Seat. Use temporary adhesive to attach the photocopy to the wood selected for the Seat.

13. Cut the Seat to the size specified on the drawing. Cut the notches in the Seat for the Arm Leg, the Left Leg and the Right Leg. Dry fit the Seat with the Chair Assembly.

14. Apply glue to the top edge of the Stretchers and clamp the Seat to the Chair Assembly.

Making the Arm Support and the Desk Top

15. Cut the Arm Support to the size specified on the drawing.

16. Cut the tenon on the Arm Support to the size specified on the drawing.

17. Apply glue and clamp the Arm Support to the Arm Leg.

18. Photocopy the drawing for the Desk Top. Use temporary adhesive to attach the photocopy to the wood selected for the Desk Top. Cut out the Desk Top, following the lines on the drawing.

19. Apply glue to the top surface of the Arm Support and the Top Support. Clamp the Desk Top to the Chair Assembly.

Finishing

20. Sand the chair and apply a finish.

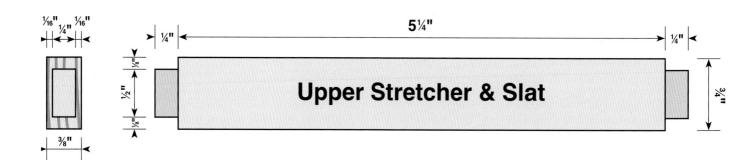

Upper Stretcher & Slat

Lower Stretcher

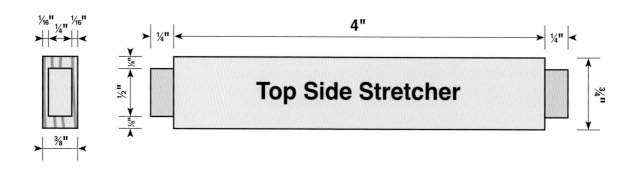

Top Side Stretcher

Bottom Side Stretcher

Shown actual size.

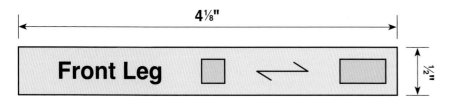

Front Leg

4⅛"

½"

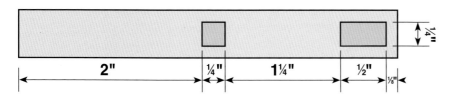

2"   ¼"   1¼"   ½"   ⅛"

¼"

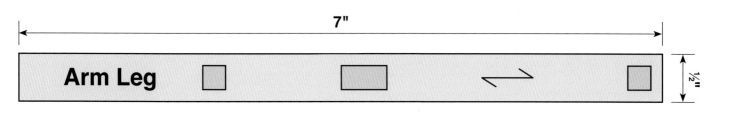

Arm Leg

7"

½"

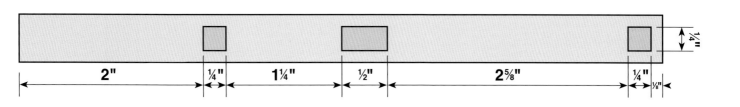

2"   ¼"   1¼"   ½"   2⅝"   ¼"   ⅛"

¼"

Shown actual size.

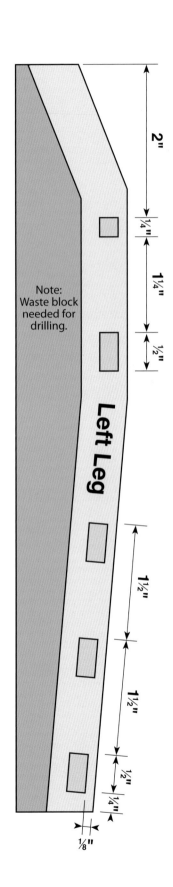

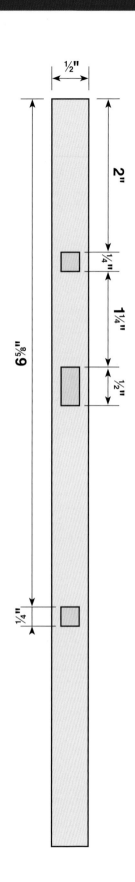

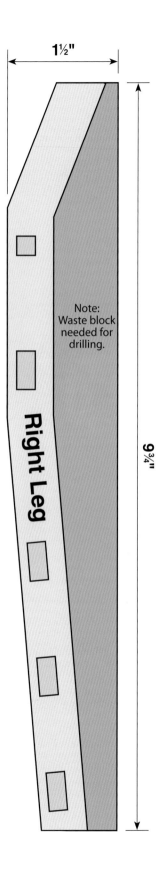

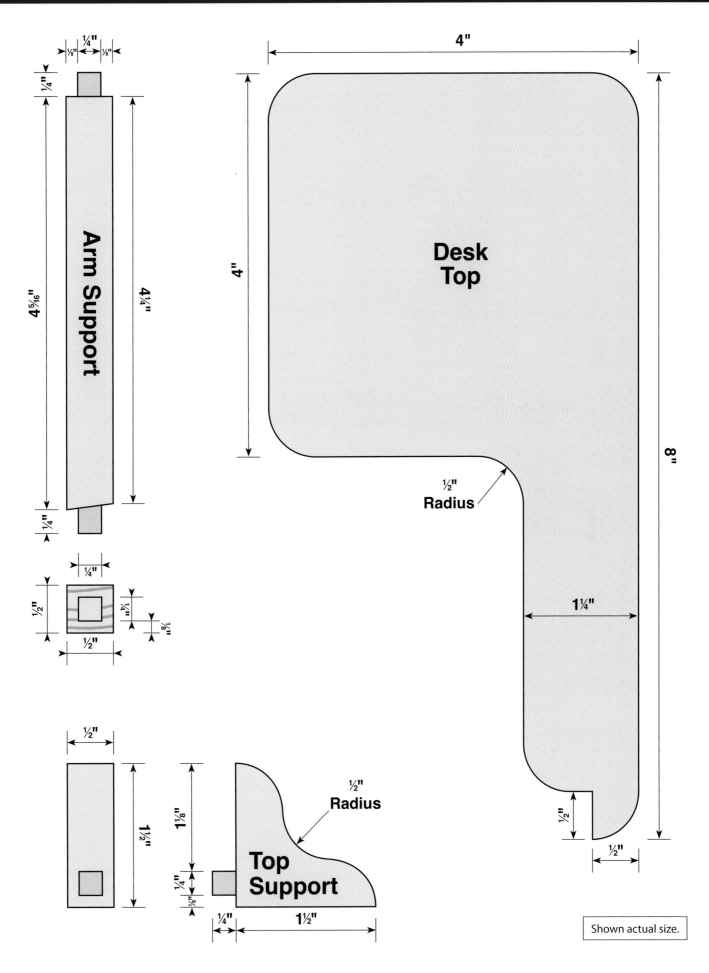

¼"
⅛" ⅛"

¼"

Arm Support

4⁵⁄₁₆"

4¼"

¼"

¼"

½"   ¼"

½"   ¼"   ⅛"

½"

4"

**Desk
Top**

4"

8"

½"
Radius

1¼"

½"

½"

½"

½"

1½"

1⅛"

¼"
⅛"

½"
Radius

**Top
Support**

¼"   1½"

Shown actual size.

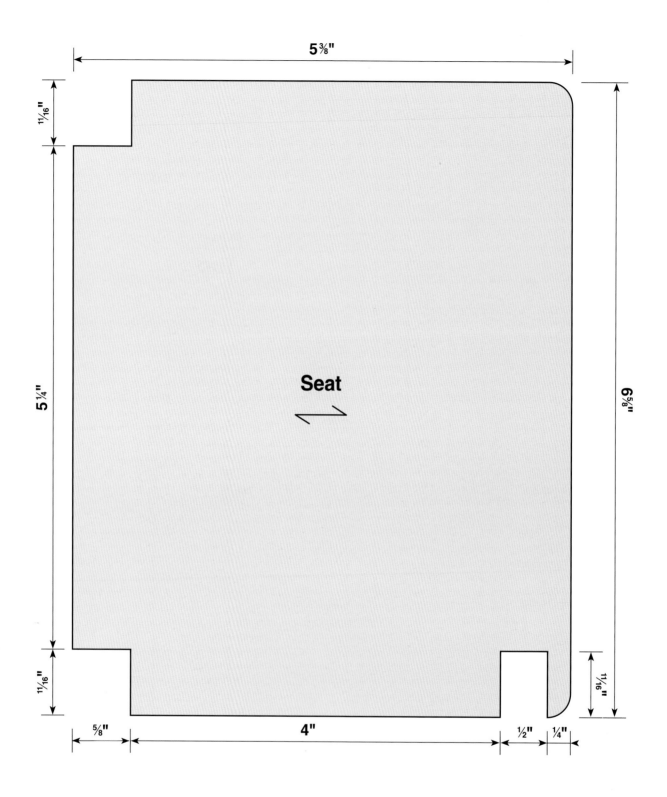

Shown actual size.

Tables

O f course, once you have a chair for your doll, you'll want a matching table to make a set. While tables are a great addition to a display of cherished dolls, they are an even greater asset to a child's collection of dolls and doll accessories. A table is an open invitation for a child to gather more dolls for play at a tea party or for an afternoon of fun at an outdoor picnic.

Here in this section, you will find four table projects: an Adirondack table, a dining table, a picnic table, and a Southwestern nightstand. The Adirondack table and the dining table are perfect matches for the Adirondack chair and the dining chair in the previous section. The picnic table is a stand-alone piece. The Southwestern nightstand will be matched up with a bed later.

When making tables, the grain pattern of the wood becomes visible in the tabletop. I recommend using a tight-grained hardwood with narrow grain lines. Gluing narrow boards together will make the tabletop look more authentic and to scale for doll-size furniture.

Page 70

Page 73

Page 77

Page 81

Adirondack Table

Materials List

Item	Width	Length	Thickness	Quantity	Material	Location
Foot & Support	½" (13mm)	4" (102mm)	¼" (6mm)	4	Fine grain pine	Page 72
Leg	1" (25mm)	5" (127mm)	¼" (6mm)	4	Fine grain pine	Page 72
Stretcher	½" (13mm)	3¼" (83mm)	¼" (6mm)	2	Fine grain pine	Page 72
Top	½" (13mm)	4½" (114mm)	¼" (6mm)	8	Fine grain pine	Page 72

Making the Table

1. Select wood materials of the proper thickness for each part. Select wood with fine grain lines in scale with this piece of furniture.

2. Lay out and cut all of the pieces to the sizes specified on the drawings.

3. Lay the eight Top pieces together in alignment, bottom sides up. Mark a line ⅜" from each end of the Top pieces. The lines represent the locations where two of the Foot & Support pieces attach to the Top pieces.

4. Glue and clamp the two Foot & Support pieces to the Top.

5. Fit and glue the two Stretchers ¾" in from each edge of the assembled Top and between the two Foot & Support pieces.

6. Glue and clamp two of the Leg pieces to each of the Foot & Support pieces. Ensure the pieces are square with the assembled Top.

7. Glue and clamp the remaining two Leg pieces to the other end of the Top Assembly.

8. Glue and clamp the Foot & Support pieces and the Stretcher pieces to the bottom of each of the Legs. Ensure they are spaced in a similar manner as the Top pieces.

9. Sand the table and apply a finish.

5"

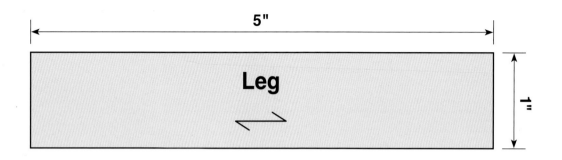

Leg

1"

3¼"

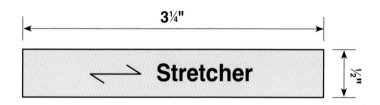

Stretcher

½"

4"

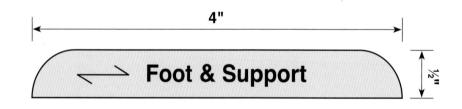

Foot & Support

½"

4½"

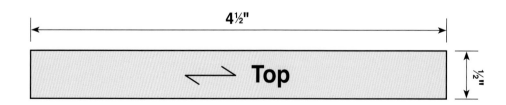

Top

½"

Shown actual size.

Dining Table

Materials List

Item	Width	Length	Thickness	Quantity	Material	Location
Leg	⅝" (16mm)	8½" (216mm)	⅝" (16mm)	4	Cherry	Page 75
Long Stretcher	1" (25mm)	11" (279mm)	½" (13mm)	2	Cherry	Page 75
Short Stretcher	1" (25mm)	6¾" (171mm)	½" (13mm)	2	Cherry	Page 75
Sub-Top	6⅜" (162mm)	10⅝" (270mm)	⅜" (10mm)	1	Cherry	No drawing
Top	8½" (216mm)	13" (330mm)	¼" (6mm)	1	Cherry	Page 76

Making the Top

1. Select wood materials of the proper thickness for each part. Select wood with fine grain lines in scale with the furniture being built.

2. Lay out and cut nine Top pieces 1" wide and 13½" long to make the Top. Match the pieces for grain pattern and color.

3. Apply glue to the edges and clamp the Top Assembly. Trim the Top Assembly to 8½" x 13" after the glue has dried.

Making the Legs and the Stretchers

4. Cut materials for the four Legs to the size specified on the drawing.

5. Lay out the location of the mortises on the Legs and cut them as indicated on the drawing. Cut two ¼" x ½" mortises, ⅜" deep, in each Leg. Mortises are cut on two sides of the Legs, 90° from each other.

6. Cut the materials for the Long Stretchers and the Short Stretchers.

7. Cut the tenons on both ends of the Stretcher pieces as specified on the drawings.

8. Dry fit the tenons on the Stretchers with the mortises in the Legs.

9. Apply glue to the tenons on the Short Stretchers and in the mortises in the Legs.

10. Assemble and clamp the pieces, ensuring the assembly is square and the unused mortises are facing the same direction.

11. Apply glue to the tenons on the Long Stretchers and in the mortises in the Legs.

12. Assemble and clamp these pieces, ensuring the assembly is square.

Making the Sub-Top

13. Cut a piece of wood to make the Sub-Top. This piece must fit snugly between the four Stretchers.

14. Apply glue to the edges of the Sub-Top and clamp it to the Leg Assembly. Ensure the Sub-Top is flush to the top surface of Stretchers.

15. Apply glue to the top surface of the Sub-Top and clamp the Top to the assembly. Ensure the Top is centered on the length and the width of the Leg Assembly.

Finishing

16. Sand the table and apply a finish.

Technical Note:
The purpose of the Sub-Top is to strengthen the Leg and the Stretcher joint and provide additional contact surface to glue the Top to the Leg Assembly. The drawing dimensions are approximate. Adjust the dimensions to match the Leg Assembly made in the previous steps.

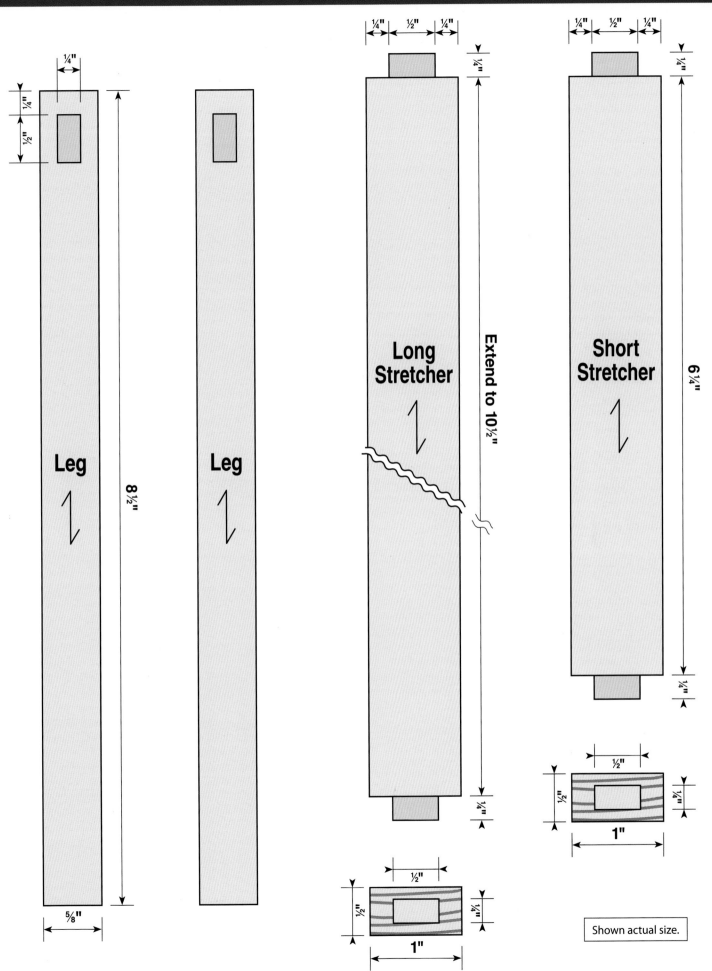

¼"

¼"

½"

Leg

8½"

⅝"

Leg

¼" ½" ¼"

¼"

Long Stretcher

Extend to 10½"

¼"

¼"

½"

½"

¼"

1"

¼" ½" ¼"

¼"

Short Stretcher

6¼"

¼"

½"

½"

¼"

1"

Shown actual size.

13"

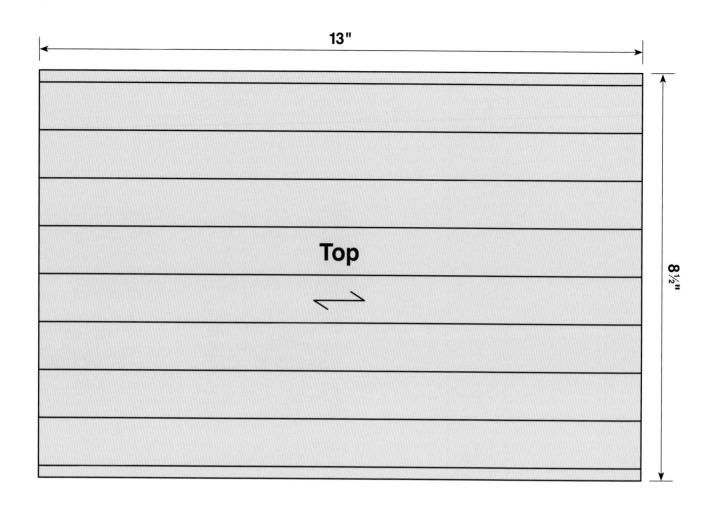

Top

8 1/2"

Enlarge 200% to
achieve actual size.

Picnic Table

Materials List

Item	Width	Length	Thickness	Quantity	Material	Location
Angle Brace	⅝" (16mm)	7" (178mm)	⅜" (10mm)	2	Birch	Page 79
End Assembly, Reference View						Page 80
Leg	1" (25mm)	9" (229mm)	⅜" (10mm)	4	Birch	Page 79
Seat	1½" (38mm)	14" (356mm)	⅜" (10mm)	2	Birch	No drawing
Seat Support	1" (25mm)	13" (330mm)	⅜" (10mm)	2	Birch	Page 79
Top	¾" (19mm)	14" (356mm)	⅜" (10mm)	8	Birch	No drawing
Top Support	1" (25mm)	7" (178mm)	⅜" (10mm)	2	Birch	Page 79

Making the Table

1. Cut all of the pieces to the sizes specified on the drawings.

2. Align the eight Top pieces. Measure and mark a line inset ¾" from each end. This line represents the location where the Top Supports attach to the Top pieces.

3. Glue and clamp the Top pieces to the Top Supports. Ensure the Tabletop Assembly is square.

4. Align the Seat boards. Measure and mark a line inset ¾" from each end. This line represents the location where the Seat Supports will attach to the Seats.

5. Glue and clamp the two Seat Supports to the Seat pieces. Ensure the Seat Assembly is square.

6. Glue and clamp the Legs to the Tabletop and Seat Assemblies, following the dimensions on the End Assembly Reference drawing.

7. Glue and clamp the Angle Braces between the Seat Supports and the Tabletop Assembly.

8. Sand the table and apply a stain and a finish.

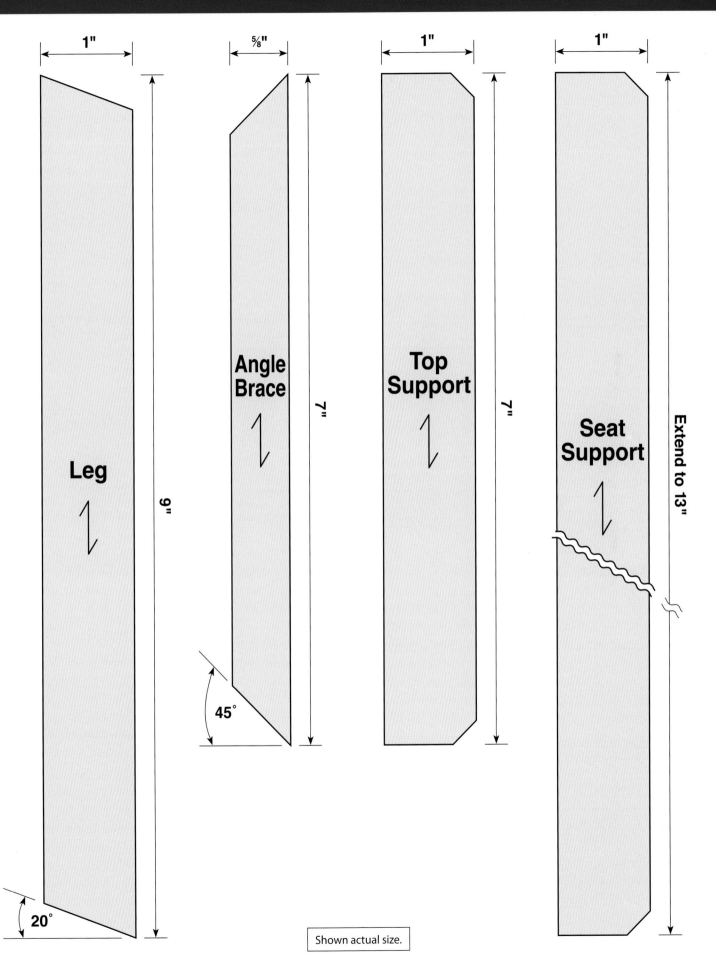

1"

⅝"

1"

1"

Leg

**Angle
Brace**

**Top
Support**

**Seat
Support**

9"

7"

7"

Extend to 13"

45°

20°

Shown actual size.

End
Assembly

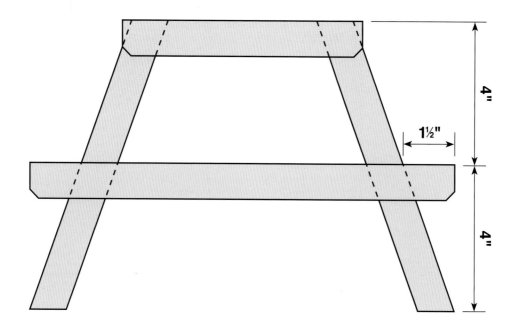

Southwestern Nightstand

Materials List

Item	Width	Length	Thickness	Quantity	Material	Location
End Insert	2¾" (70mm)	3" (76mm)	¼" (6mm)	2	Birch	Page 83
End Stretcher	½" (13mm)	2¾" (70mm)	⅜" (10mm)	2	Cherry	Page 83
Front Stretcher	½" (13mm)	3½" (89mm)	⅜" (10mm)	2	Cherry	Page 83
Leg	½" (13mm)	4" (102mm)	½" (13mm)	4	Cherry	Page 83
Top	4" (102mm)	4½" (114mm)	⅜" (10mm)	1	Birch	No drawing

Making the Table

1. Select wood materials of the proper thickness for each part. Select wood with fine grain lines in scale with the furniture being built.

2. Lay out and cut all of the pieces to the sizes specified on the drawings.

3. Lay out the location and cut ⅜" deep mortises in each Leg as specified on the drawing.

4. Lay out and cut tenons on both ends of the Front Stretchers as specified on the drawing.

5. Dry fit the tenons and mortises.

6. Photocopy the pattern for the Front Stretchers. Use temporary adhesive to attach the photocopy to the board. Cut out the decorative diamond on these pieces.

7. Photocopy the pattern for the End Inserts. Use temporary adhesive to attach the photocopy to the board. Cut out the two End Inserts.

8. Cut the two End Stretchers to the width specified on the drawing and slightly longer than the length indicated on the drawing.

9. Glue and clamp the End Stretcher to the bottom end of the End Insert. Ensure these are flush with the back surface and centered on the width of the End Insert. After the glue has dried, trim the End Stretcher flush with the End Insert.

10. Glue and clamp the End Insert between two of the Legs. Align this flush with the top of the Legs and flush with the inside edge of the Legs. Ensure the mortises on both Legs are facing to the inside.

11. Glue and clamp the Front Stretchers and the Back Stretchers between the Leg Assemblies. Ensure the assembly is square.

12. Glue and clamp the Top to the Leg Assembly.

13. Sand the table and apply a finish.

> **Technical Note:**
> The Top will look more authentic if it is made from four 1"-wide pieces of wood glued together to form the 4"-wide Top.

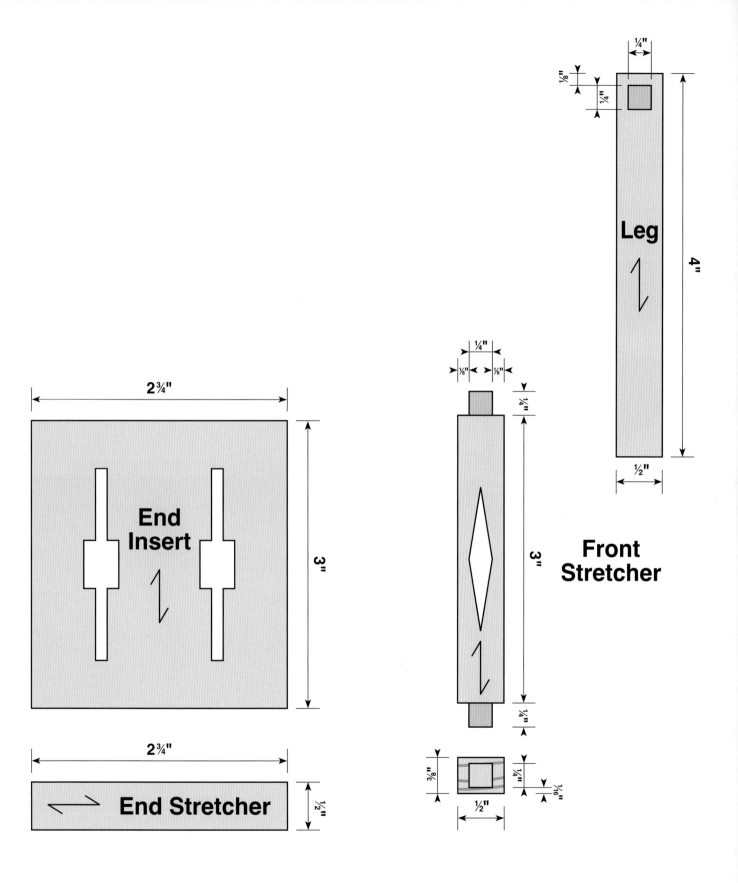

**End
Insert**

2¾"

3"

End Stretcher

2¾"

½"

Leg

4"

¼"

⅛"

¼"

½"

**Front
Stretcher**

¼"

⅛"   ⅛"

¼"

3"

¼"

⅜"

½"

¼"

1/16"

Shown actual size.

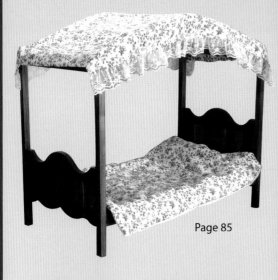

Page 85

Page 93

Page 97

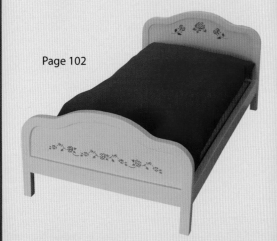

Page 102

Beds

Now that I've introduced the idea of a bedroom suite in the previous chapter with the plans for the Southwestern Nightstand, let's focus on making types of beds for dolls. Here in this section, you will find projects for four beds: the Canopy Bed, Bunk Bed, Southwestern Bed, and Classic Bed. These beds can be matched up with a variety of furniture in this book to create beautiful bedrooms that are equally suited to display or play.

When creating beds make a tight joint between the head, footboards, and side rails. This is the critical area with the highest stress. A square should be used at assembly to help ensure the side rails are square with the head and footboards. Personalize these beds by choosing paint colors and blanket fabrics that match the owner's bed.

Canopy Bed

Materials List

Item	Width	Length	Thickness	Quantity	Material	Location
Canopy End	1¼" (32mm)	11" (279mm)	½" (13mm)	2	Walnut	Page 88
Canopy Side	4⅝" (117mm)	22" (559mm)	½" (13mm)	2	Walnut	Page 89
Dowel Rods	¼" (6mm)	11" (279mm)	¼" (6mm)	3	Walnut Dowel	No drawing
End Bottom	1¼" (32mm)	11" (279mm)	½" (13mm)	2	Walnut	Page 90
End Top	2" (51mm)	11" (279mm)	½" (13mm)	2	Walnut	Page 90
Foot Insert Panel	2¾" (70mm)	10½" (267mm)	¼" (6mm)	1	Walnut	No drawing
Foot Post Left	⅝" (16mm)	16½" (419mm)	⅝" (16mm)	1	Walnut	Page 91
Foot Post Right	⅝" (16mm)	16½" (419mm)	⅝" (16mm)	1	Walnut	Page 91
Head Insert Panel	4½" (114mm)	10½" (267mm)	¼" (6mm)	1	Walnut	No drawing
Head Post Left	⅝" (16mm)	16½" (419mm)	⅝" (16mm)	1	Walnut	Page 92
Head Post Right	⅝" (16mm)	16½" (419mm)	⅝" (16mm)	1	Walnut	Page 92
Mattress Support	10⅞" (276mm)	21½" (546mm)	¼" (6mm)	1	Plywood	No drawing
Side Rail	1¼" (32mm)	22" (559mm)	½" (13mm)	2	Walnut	Page 88

Making the Bed End Assembly

1. Select hardwood materials of the proper thickness for each bed part on the materials list.

2. Cut ¼" x ¼" dado grooves on the edges of the End Top and the End Bottom boards, as marked on the drawing.

3. Cut the End Top, the End Bottom, and the Canopy End pieces to the widths and lengths specified on the drawings.

4. Lay out and cut the tenons on both ends of these pieces to the dimensions specified on the drawings.

5. Cut the ⅝" x ⅝" Head Post to the length specified on the drawings.

6. Lay out the location of the mortises specified on the drawings for the Head Post Left and the Head Post Right.

7. Use a ¼" mortise drill and cut all of the mortises to ⅜" deep and to the lengths specified on the drawings.

8. Dry assemble the tenons on these pieces with the matching mortises in the Post.

9. Lay out and cut the Head Insert Panel to the size specified on the drawing.

10. Dry assemble the Head Insert Panel with the End Top and the End Bottom pieces.

11. Photocopy the patterns for the End Top and the End Bottom pieces. Use a temporary adhesive to attach the photocopies to these pieces and cut the decorative profiles. Sand the edges of these pieces. Dry assemble the Headboard Assembly.

Technical Note:
The End Top and the End Bottom pieces are too small to handle safely when cutting the dados. To make this operation safer, use a 4"-wide by 22"-long board. Cut the dado on the entire length of the board before cutting the pieces to their final widths and lengths. This improves the safety of the dado operation.

12. Apply glue to the tenons on the Canopy End, the End Top, and the End Bottom and to the mortises on the Post.

13. Assemble the Head Insert Panel with the End Top and the End Bottom pieces.

14. Insert the tenons of these pieces into the mortises in the Head Post Left and the Head Post Right. Clamp the Headboard Assembly. Ensure the Headboard Assembly is square.

15. Follow the same steps outlined above to make the Footboard Assembly.

Making the Mattress Support System

16. Cut a board 3" wide and 22" long for the Side Rail pieces.

17. Cut a ¼" x ⅛" dado groove in both edges of this board.

18. Cut the two Side Rail pieces to the width and length specified on the drawing.

19. Cut tenons on both ends of these pieces to the size specified on the drawing.

20. Dry assemble the Side Rail tenons to the mortises in the Head Post Left, the Foot Post Left, the Head Post Right, and the Foot Post Right. Adjust the tenon dimensions by using a file, if needed.

21. Cut the Mattress Support to the dimensions specified on the materials list.

22. Dry assemble the Mattress Support System to the Headboard and Footboard Assemblies. Do not glue any of these pieces yet.

23. Select a piece of wood with clear, straight grain to be used for the Canopy Sides.

24. The board should be at least 4⅝" wide and have one straight edge.

25. Cut the board to 22" long, with both ends square to the straight edge.

26. Cut the tenons on both ends of both pieces to the dimensions specified on the drawings.

27. Photocopy the patterns for the Canopy Sides (left and right). Match up the patterns to create the entire Canopy Side pattern and ensure the pattern is the correct length of 22". Use temporary adhesive to attach the photocopy to a scrap piece of ¼" plywood to make a test pattern. Test cut the Canopy Sides, following the photocopied lines.

28. Dry assemble the test pattern with all of the other pieces of the Bed Assembly. If the test pattern does not provide a satisfactory fit, adjust the pattern as needed.

29. Drill small holes in the test pattern where the Dowel Rods will be located.

30. Lay out the Canopy Sides using the test pattern. Mark the location for the Dowel Rods.

31. Drill three ¼"-diameter holes ¼" deep at the marked locations for the Dowel Rods.

32. Cut out the Canopy Sides from walnut.

33. Smooth out the profile edges on the Canopy Sides using a spindle sander.

34. Cut three ¼"-diameter Dowel Rods to the length specified on the materials list.

35. Dry assemble the Canopy Sides with the Dowel Rods to all other pieces of the Bed Assembly.

Assembling the Canopy Sides and the Mattress Support System

36. Apply glue to the tenons on the Side Rails, the Canopy Sides, and the mortises in the Head Posts and the Foot Posts.

37. Apply glue to the dado grooves in the Side Rails and assemble the Mattress Support into the Side Rails.

38. Insert the Dowel Rods between the Canopy Sides.

39. Insert the tenons of all of these pieces into the mortises in the Head Posts and the Foot Posts.

40. Ensure the Bed Assembly is square.

41. Clamp the assembly until the glue is dry.

Finishing

42. Sand the bed and apply a stain and a finish.

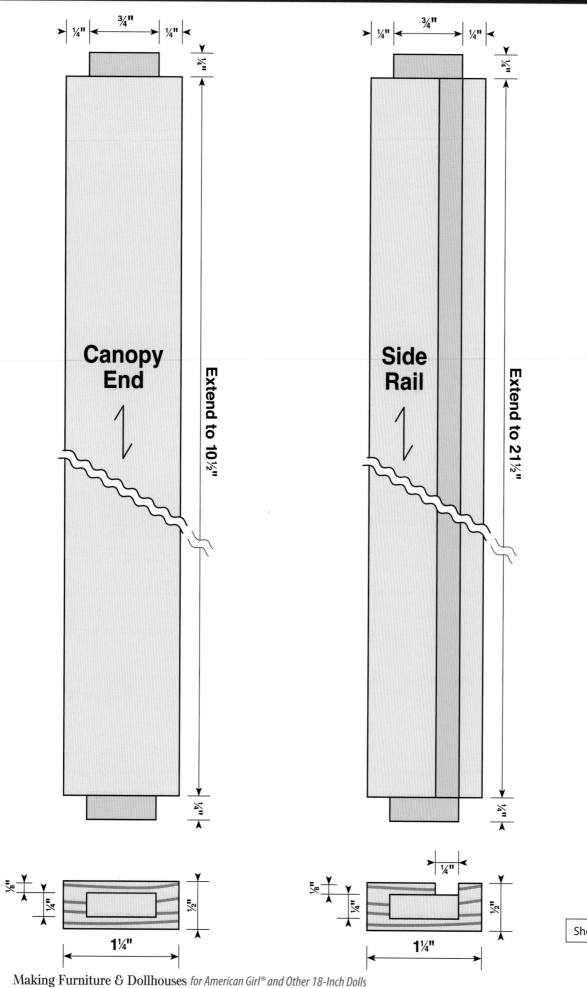

¾" ¼" ¼" ¼"

Canopy End

Extend to 10½"

¼"

Side Rail

Extend to 21½"

¼"

⅛" ¼" ½" 1¼"

⅛" ¼" ½" 1¼" ¼"

Shown actual size.

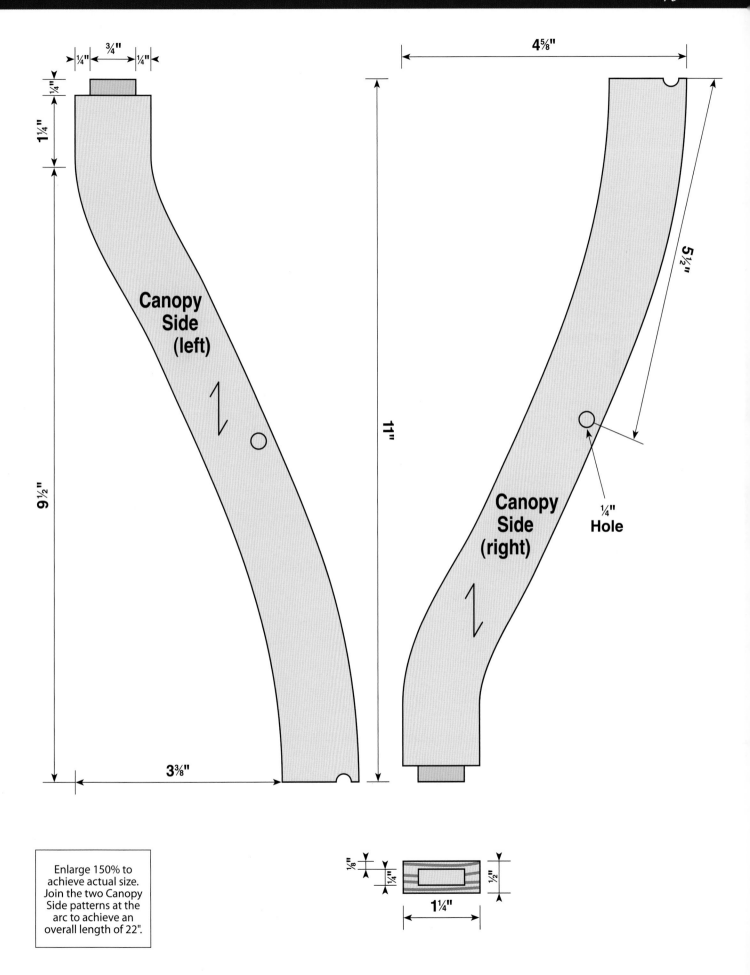

¾"
¼" ¼"
¼"
1¼"

4⅝"

11"

5½"

Canopy Side (left)

Canopy Side (right)

¼" Hole

9½"

3⅜"

Enlarge 150% to achieve actual size. Join the two Canopy Side patterns at the arc to achieve an overall length of 22".

⅛"
¼"
½"
1¼"

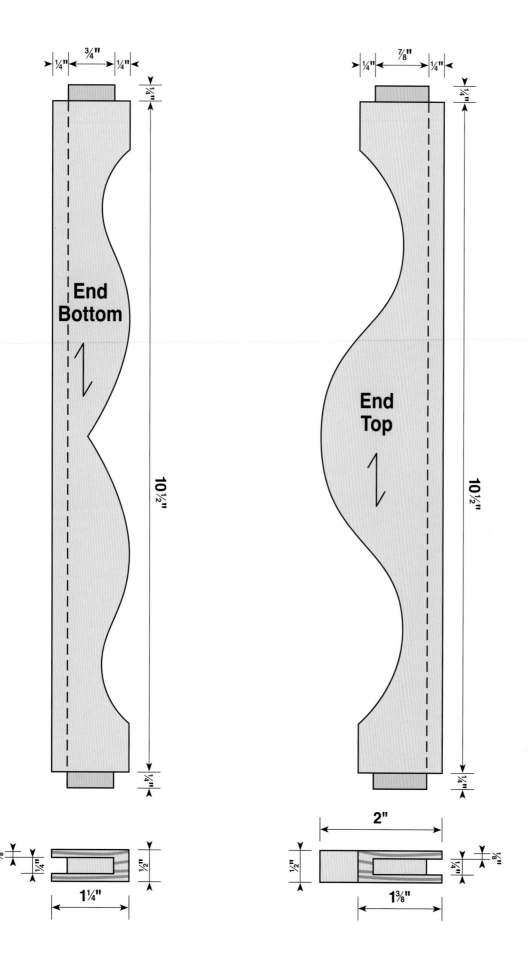

End Bottom

End Top

¾"

¼" ¼"

⅞"

¼" ¼"

¼"

¼"

10½"

10½"

¼"

¼"

⅛"

¼"

½"

1¼"

2"

½"

⅛"

¼"

1⅜"

Enlarge 150% to achieve actual size.

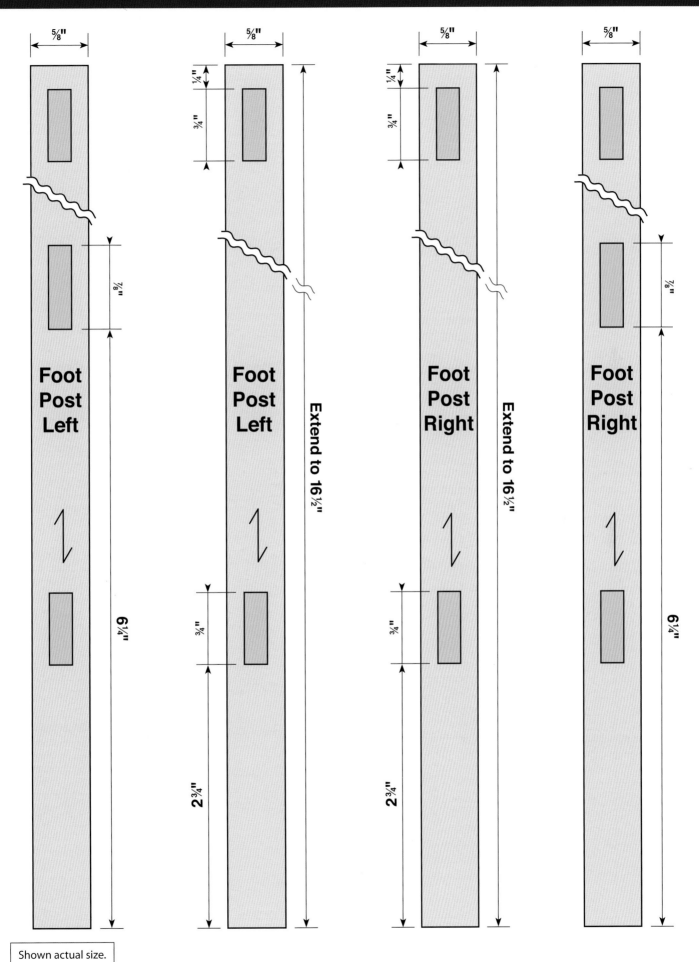

5/8"

1/4"

3/4"

7/8"

Foot Post Left

Foot Post Left

Foot Post Right

Foot Post Right

Extend to 16½"

Extend to 16½"

6¼"

2¾"

2¾"

6¼"

Shown actual size.

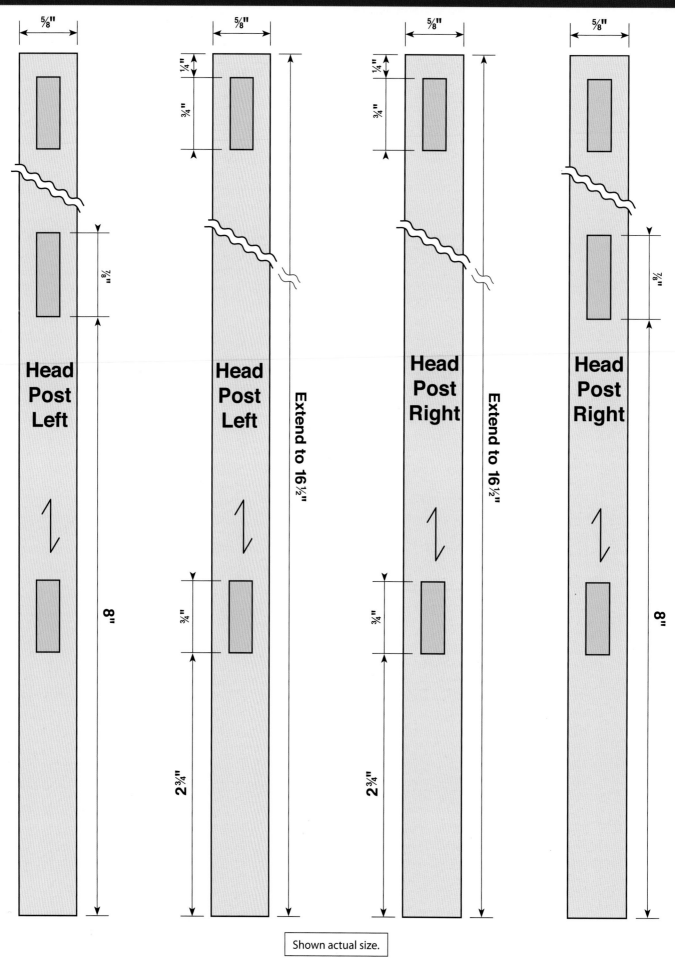

Head Post Left

Head Post Left — Extend to 16½"

Head Post Right — Extend to 16½"

Head Post Right

⅝"

¼"

¾"

⅞"

8"

2¾"

Shown actual size.

Bunk Bed

Materials List

Item	Width	Length	Thickness	Quantity	Material	Location
Bottom End Rail	1¼" (32mm)	10½" (267mm)	½" (13mm)	4	Hardwood	Page 96
End Panel	4¾" (121mm)	10" (254mm)	¼" (6mm)	4	Plywood	No drawing
Mattress Support	10¾" (273mm)	21½" (546mm)	¼" (6mm)	1	Plywood	No drawing
Post Left	¾" (19mm)	21¾" (552mm)	¾" (19mm)	2	Hardwood	Page 95
Post Right	¾" (19mm)	21¾" (552mm)	¾" (19mm)	2	Hardwood	Page 95
Side Rail	1¼" (32mm)	21½" (546mm)	½" (13mm)	2	Hardwood	Page 96
Top End Rail	¾" (19mm)	10½" (267mm)	½" (13mm)	4	Hardwood	Page 96

Making the Bed End Assembly

1. Select hardwood materials of the proper thickness for each bed part.

2. Cut two pieces of ½"-thick wood, 2" wide and 21" long.

3. Cut dado grooves on the edge of these boards as specified on the drawings for the Top End Rails and the Bottom End Rails.

4. Using the board above, cut the End Rail pieces to the widths and lengths specified on the drawings.

5. Cut tenons on each end of the End Rail pieces as specified on the drawing.

6. Cut four Posts to the specified sizes.

7. Lay out the locations of the mortises as specified on the drawings for the Post Left and the Post Right.

8. Using a ¼" mortise drill, cut all of the mortises ⅜" deep.

9. Dry assemble the End Rail tenons with the mortises in the Posts.

10. Cut the four End Panels from ¼" plywood.

11. Apply glue to the End Rail tenons and the Post Left and Post Right mortises.

12. Clamp two of the End Panels with one Left Post and one Right Post. Ensure the Bed End Assembly is square.

13. Repeat the steps outlined above for the second Bed End Assembly.

Making the Mattress Support System

14. Cut a board 2½" wide and 21½" long for the Side Rails.

15. Cut ¼" x ¼" dado grooves on both edges of the board.

16. Cut the Side Rails from this board to the width and length specified on drawing.

17. Cut tenons on each end of the Side Rails as specified on the drawing.

18. Cut the Mattress Support to size as specified on the materials list.

19. Dry assemble the Side Rail tenons to the mortises in the Bed End Assemblies.

Assembling the Bed End Assemblies to the Side Rails

20. Apply glue to the tenons on the Side Rails and the mortises in the Bed End Assemblies.

21. Apply glue to the dado grooves in the Side Rails and assemble the Mattress Support with the Side Rails.

22. Insert the tenons of the Side Rails into the mortises on the Bed End Assemblies.

23. Assemble both upper and lower Mattress Support Assemblies with both Bed End Assemblies.

24. Ensure the assembly is square.

25. Clamp the assembled bed until the glue is dry.

Finishing

26. Sand the bed and apply a finish.

27. Apply stencils (available at hobby and craft stores in miniature sizes) as desired.

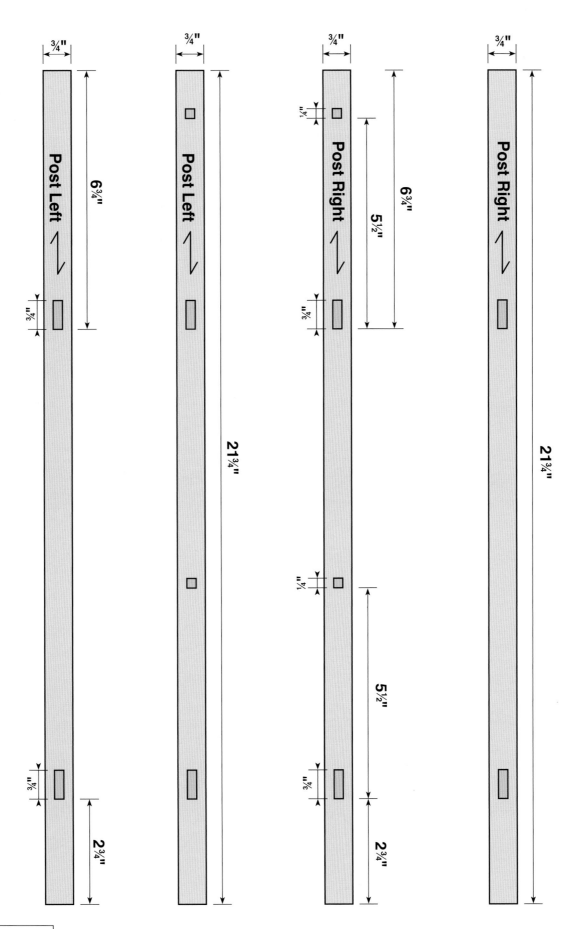

Enlarge 250% to achieve actual size.

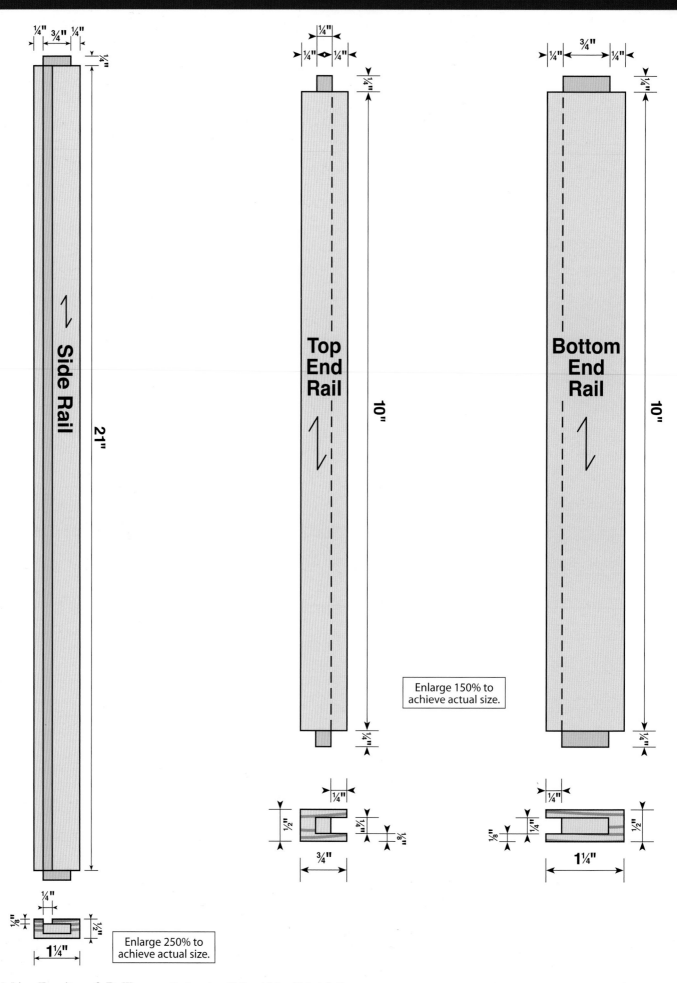

¼" ¾" ¼"

¼"

Side Rail

21"

¼"

¼" ¼"

Top End Rail

10"

¼"

¾" ¼"

¼"

Bottom End Rail

10"

¼"

Enlarge 150% to achieve actual size.

¼"

½"

¼"

⅛"

¾"

¼"

⅛"

¼"

½"

1¼"

¼"

⅛"

½"

1¼"

Enlarge 250% to achieve actual size.

Southwestern Bed

Materials List

Item	Width	Length	Thickness	Quantity	Material	Location
Footboard	4⅜" (111mm)	10½" (267mm)	⅜" (10mm)	1	Poplar	Page 99
Headboard	6½" (165mm)	10½" (267mm)	⅜" (10mm)	1	Poplar	Page 100
Long Post	½" (13mm)	7" (178mm)	½" (13mm)	2	Cherry	Page 101
Mattress Support	11" (279mm)	21" (533mm)	¼" (6mm)	1	Plywood	No drawing
Short Post	½" (13mm)	5¼" (133mm)	½" (13mm)	2	Cherry	Page 101
Side Rail	1¼" (32mm)	21½" (546mm)	½" (13mm)	2	Poplar	Page 101

Making the Bed End Assembly

1. Select hardwood materials of the proper thickness for each bed part on the materials list.

2. Cut the Long Post to the dimensions specified on drawing.

3. Lay out the locations of the mortises as specified on the drawing for the Long Post.

4. Using a ¼" mortise drill and mortise attachment, drill all mortises ⅜" deep.

5. Photocopy the pattern for the Headboard. Using temporary adhesive, attach the copy to the ⅜"-thick wood selected for the Headboard.

6. Drill pilot holes on the Headboard for all of the inside cuts to prepare the piece for the scroll saw.

7. Cut out the Headboard using a scroll saw.

8. Ensure the end cuts on the length of the Headboard are straight and square.

9. Measure and mark the Long Post 1¼" from the bottom. This is the location where the Headboard will attach to the Long Post.

10. Apply glue to the ends of the Headboard and clamp it to the Long Post. Ensure the ⅜"-thick Headboard is centered on the ½" thickness of the Long Post and aligned with the marks. Ensure the mortises are both located on the same side of the Headboard Assembly.

11. Follow the same steps outlined above to make the Footboard Assembly.

Making the Mattress Support System

12. Cut a board 3" wide and 21½" long for the Side Rail pieces.

13. Cut a ¼" x ⅛" dado groove on both edges of this board.

14. From the 3" board, cut the Side Rail pieces to the width and length specified on drawing.

15. Cut the tenons on each end of the Side Rails to the size specified on the drawing.

16. From ¼" plywood, cut the Mattress Support to the dimensions specified on the materials list.

17. Dry assemble the Side Rails and the Mattress Support to the Post. (Adjust the tenon dimensions with a file if needed.)

Assembling the Headboard and Footboard Assemblies to the Side Rails

18. Apply glue to the tenons on each Side Rail and to the mortises in the Long Posts.

19. Apply glue in the dado grooves in the Side Rails.

20. Assemble the Mattress Support with the Side Rails.

21. Insert the Side Rail tenons into the mortises on the Long Posts of the Headboard Assembly. Clamp the assembly until the glue is dry.

22. Ensure that the assembly is square.

23. Follow the same steps outlined above to assemble the Footboard to the Side Rails.

Finishing

24. Sand the bed and apply a finish.

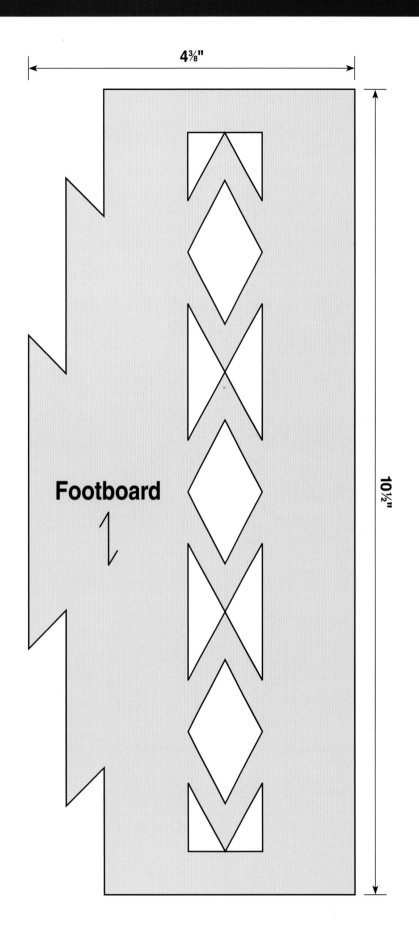

4⅜"

10½"

Footboard

Enlarge 125% to achieve actual size.

6½"

10½"

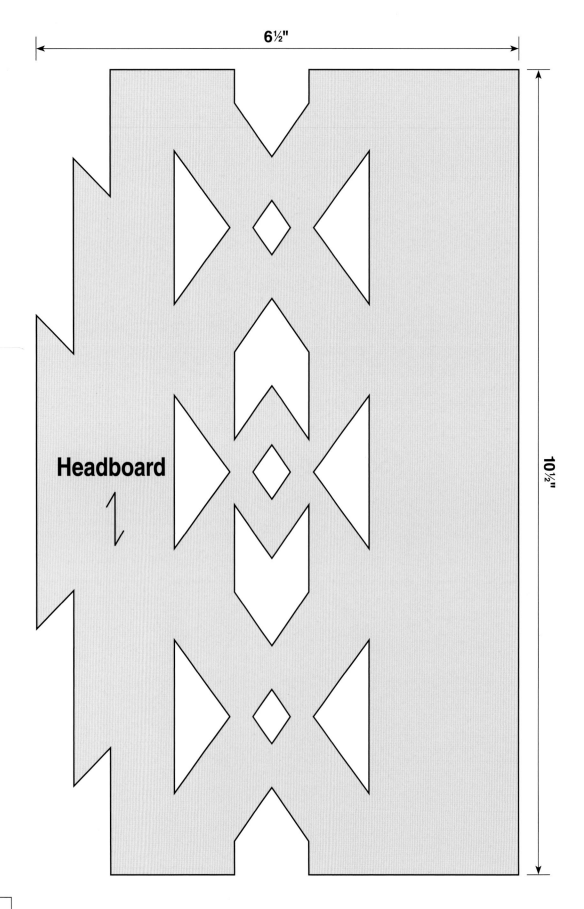

Headboard

Enlarge 125% to
achieve actual size.

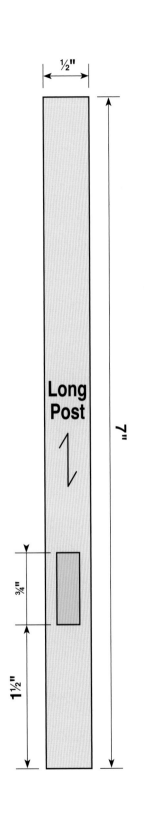

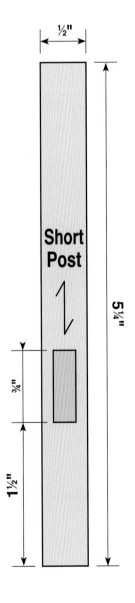

½"

Long
Post

7"

¾"

1½"

½"

Short
Post

5¼"

¾"

1½"

¼"   ¾"   ¼"

¼"

Side
Rail

Extend to 21"

¼"

¼"

¼"

½"

1¼"

Shown actual size.

Classic Bed

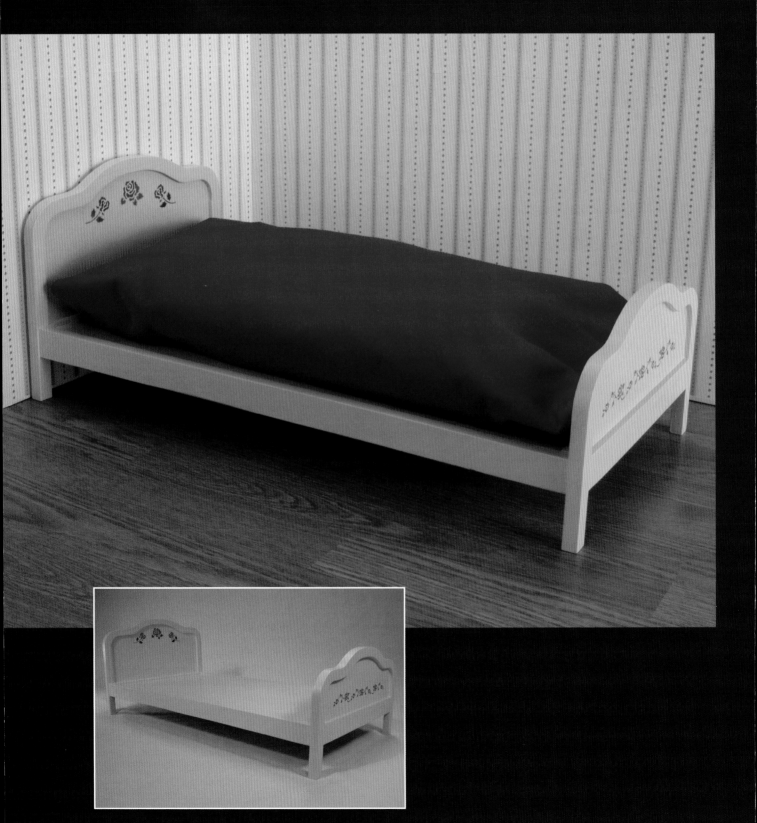

Materials List

Item	Width	Length	Thickness	Quantity	Material	Location
End Rail	1¼" (32mm)	10½" (267mm)	½" (13mm)	2	Poplar	Page 105
Foot Leg	⅝" (16mm)	4" (102mm)	½" (13mm)	2	Poplar	No drawing
Foot Panel	3¼" (83mm)	10¼" (260mm)	¼" (6mm)	1	Poplar	Page 107
Head Leg	⅝" (16mm)	6" (152mm)	½" (13mm)	2	Poplar	No drawing
Head Panel	5⅛" (130mm)	10¼" (260mm)	¼" (6mm)	1	Poplar	Page 107
Mattress Support	11" (279mm)	20½" (521mm)	¼" (6mm)	1	Plywood	No drawing
Side Rail	1¼" (32mm)	21" (533mm)	½" (13mm)	2	Poplar	Page 105
Stretcher	1¼" (32mm)	10¼" (260mm)	½" (13mm)	2	Poplar	No drawing
Top	3" (76mm)	11½" (292mm)	½" (13mm)	2	Poplar	Page 106

Making the Mattress Support System

1. Select wood materials of the proper thickness for each bed part on the materials list.

2. Cut two boards to a width of 2½" and a length of 21" to be used for the Side Rail and the End Rail pieces.

3. Cut ¼" x ¼" dado grooves on both edges of these boards as specified on the drawings.

4. Cut the Side Rail and the End Rail pieces to the widths and lengths specified on drawings.

5. Cut the Mattress Support to the size specified on the materials list.

6. Dry fit the Mattress Support, End Rails, and Side Rails. The End Rails fit between the Side Rails and are flush with the ends of the Side Rails.

7. Apply glue to the ends of the End Rails and in the dado groove of the Side Rails.

8. Glue and clamp the assembly and the Mattress Support.

9. Ensure the End Rail pieces are flush and square with the ends of the Side Rails.

Making the Headboard and Footboard Assemblies

10. Photocopy the pattern for the Top twice. Use temporary adhesive to attach the photocopies to the wood selected for these parts.

11. Cut the two Top pieces, following the lines on the photocopied pattern.

12. Sand the edges of the pieces to remove any imperfections in the cutting.

13. Photocopy the pattern for the Head Panel. Use temporary adhesive to attach the photocopy to the wood selected for the Head Panel.

14. Use the Top piece (cut in the previous steps) to check the fit of the inside of the Top piece and the corresponding curved sections on the paper pattern. Re-mark the paper pattern, if necessary.

15. Cut out the Head Panel by carefully following the lines on the photocopied pattern.

16. Glue and clamp the Top piece to the Head Panel. Ensure the Top piece is flush with one face of the Head Panel.

17. Cut the Stretcher to the dimensions specified on the drawing.

18. Glue and clamp the Stretcher to the bottom of the Head Panel. Ensure the Stretcher is flush with the face of the Head Panel.

19. Cut the Head Legs to the size specified on the drawing.

20. Glue and clamp the Head Legs to each side of the Headboard Assembly.

21. Follow the same steps outlined above to make the Footboard Assembly.

Assembling the Bed

22. Dry assemble the Headboard Assembly to the Mattress Support.

23. Check to ensure the Headboard Assembly is square when it is clamped to the Mattress Support System. If it is not square, adjust the fit of the Side Rails using a disc sander.

24. Glue and clamp the Headboard Assembly to the Mattress Support System.

25. Ensure the bottoms of the Side Rails align with the bottom of the Stretcher on the Headboard Assembly.

26. Follow the same steps outlined above to attach the Footboard Assembly to the Mattress Support.

Finishing

27. Sand the bed and apply a finish.

28. Stencils in miniature sizes are available at hobby and craft stores.

Technical Note:
Ensure that the length of the Stretcher specified on the drawing matches the length of the Head Panel made above. If the cut result is different than that specified on the drawing, adjust the length as necessary.

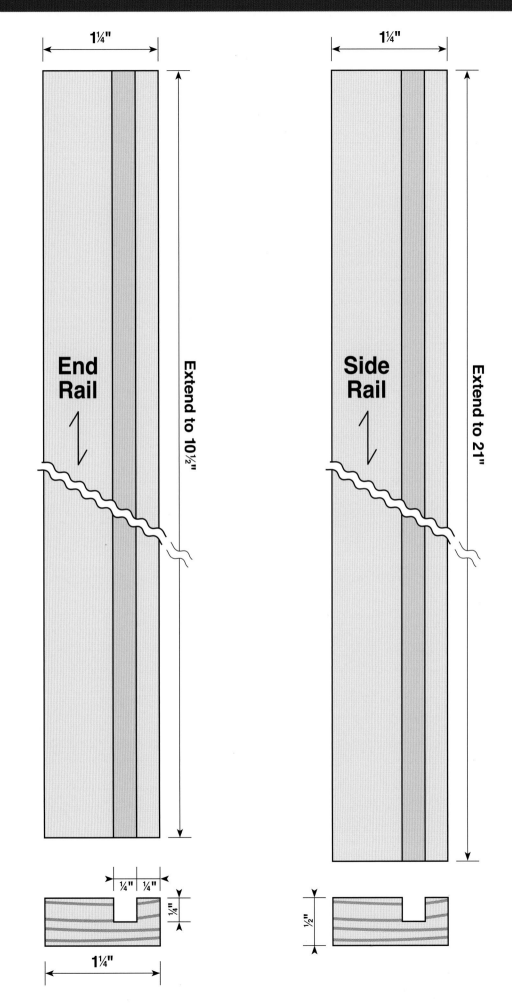

1¼"

End Rail

Extend to 10½"

1¼"

Side Rail

Extend to 21"

Shown actual size.

¼" ¼"

¼"

1¼"

½"

3"

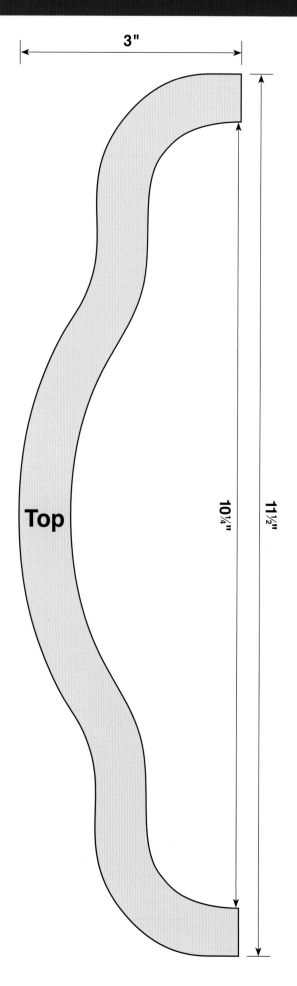

Top

10¼"

11½"

Enlarge 125% to achieve actual size.

5⅛"

10¼"

Head Panel

Foot Panel

3¼"

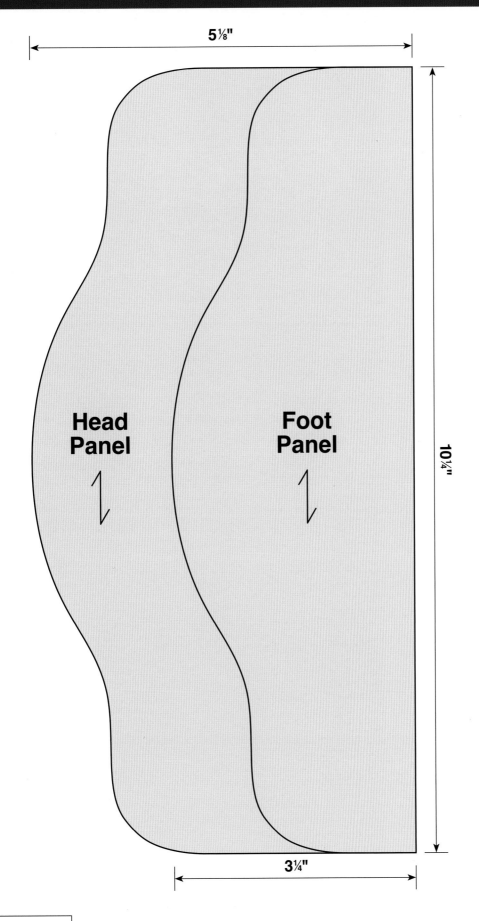

Enlarge 125% to achieve actual size.

Page 109

Page 118

Page 126

Page 135

Dressers & Chests

What bedroom suite would be complete without a dresser or chest in which to store the many clothes and accessories dolls seem to accumulate? Here in this chapter, you will find plans for four dressers and chests: the Tall Dresser, Short Dresser, Armoire, and Treasure Chest.

Essentially, dressers and chests are boxes with simple glue joints. The important focus is to make the drawers square and sized to operate smoothly. The drawers are made with plywood except for the fronts. The tops and armoire panels could be made by gluing narrow boards together to create a look more authentic and to scale for doll-size furniture.

Tall Dresser

Materials List

Item	Width	Length	Thickness	Quantity	Material	Location
Back	10¼" (260mm)	10½" (267mm)	¼" (6mm)	1	Walnut	No drawing
Back Leg	½" (13mm)	11" (279mm)	½" (13mm)	2	Walnut	Page 114
Bottom Stretcher	1" (25mm)	10¼" (260mm)	⅜" (10mm)	1	Walnut	Page 113
Chest Top	6" (152mm)	11¼" (285mm)	⅜" (10mm)	1	Walnut	No drawing
Drawer Back #1	1" (25mm)	9¼" (235mm)	¼" (6mm)	1	Plywood	Page 116
Drawer Back #2	1½" (38mm)	9¼" (235mm)	¼" (6mm)	1	Plywood	Page 116
Drawer Back #3	2¼" (57mm)	9¼" (235mm)	¼" (6mm)	1	Plywood	Page 116
Drawer Back #4	2¾" (70mm)	9¼" (235mm)	¼" (6mm)	1	Plywood	Page 116
Drawer Bottom	4¾" (121mm)	9¾" (248mm)	¼" (6mm)	4	Plywood	No drawing
Drawer Front #1	1¼" (32mm)	9¾" (248mm)	⅜" (10mm)	1	Walnut	Page 114
Drawer Front #2	1¾" (44mm)	9¾" (248mm)	⅜" (10mm)	1	Walnut	Page 114
Drawer Front #3	2½" (64mm)	9¾" (248mm)	⅜" (10mm)	1	Walnut	Page 114
Drawer Front #4	3" (76mm)	9¾" (248mm)	⅜" (10mm)	1	Walnut	Page 114
Drawer Side #1	1" (25mm)	4¾" (121mm)	¼" (6mm)	2	Plywood	Page 116
Drawer Side #2	1½" (38mm)	4¾" (121mm)	¼" (6mm)	2	Plywood	Page 116
Drawer Side #3	2¼" (57mm)	4¾" (121mm)	¼" (6mm)	2	Plywood	Page 116
Drawer Side #4	2¾" (70mm)	4¾" (121mm)	¼" (6mm)	2	Plywood	Page 116
Drawer Support Panel	4¼" (108mm)	9¾" (248mm)	¼" (6mm)	5	Walnut	Page 117
Insert Panel	4 ¼" (108mm)	10" (254mm)	¼" (6mm)	2	Walnut	No drawing
Left Leg	1½" (38mm)	11" (279mm)	½" (13mm)	1	Walnut	Page 115
Right Leg	1½" (38mm)	11" (279mm)	½" (13mm)	1	Walnut	Page 115
Side Panel Assembly						Page 113
Side Rail	⅝" (16mm)	4¼" (108mm)	⅜" (10mm)	2	Walnut	Page 117
Support Stretcher	⅝" (16mm)	10¼" (260mm)	⅜" (10mm)	4	Walnut	Page 117
Wood Knobs			⅝" (16mm) Dia.	8		No drawing

Making the Side Panel Assemblies

1. Select hardwood materials of the proper thickness for each part.

2. Cut the material to the sizes specified on the drawings for the Left Leg and the Right Leg.

3. Photocopy the drawings for the Legs. Use temporary adhesive to attach the photocopy to the wood.

4. Lay out the locations of the mortises as specified on the drawings for the Left Leg and the Right Leg.

5. Use a ¼" mortise drill to cut all mortises to ⅜" deep and to the lengths specified on the drawings. *Do not cut the decorative shape on the front edge of these Legs at this time.*

6. Cut a ½"-thick board to 11" long and an oversized width. This board will be used to make the Back Legs.

7. Cut a rabbet on both edges (on the oversized-width board) as specified on the drawing for the Back Legs.

8. From the oversized board, cut the Back Leg pieces to the width specified on the drawing.

9. Cut the Insert Panel pieces to the size specified on the drawing.

10. Cut the Side Rail pieces to the size specified on the drawing.

11. Apply glue to the end of the Insert Panel and clamp it to the Side Rail. Ensure the Side Rail is flush with the face of the Insert Panel.

12. Apply glue to the edge of the Insert Panel and clamp it to the Left Front Leg. Ensure the Insert Panel is flush with the side of the Front Leg with mortises and flush with the top end of the Front Leg.

13. Apply glue to the edge of the Insert Panel and clamp it to the Back Leg. Ensure the Insert Panel is flush with the inside and top of the Back Leg. Reference the Left Side Assembly drawing for proper orientation of the Back Leg.

14. Use the same procedure outlined above to assemble the Right Side Assembly.

Making the Chest Assembly

15. Cut the Support Stretcher and the Bottom Stretcher pieces to the sizes specified on the drawings.

16. Lay out and cut the tenons on these pieces as specified on the drawings.

17. Dry fit the tenons into the mortises in the Left Side Assembly and the Right Side Assembly.

18. Photocopy the drawing for the Bottom Stretcher. Use temporary adhesive to attach the photocopied pattern to the Bottom Stretcher and cut out the decorative shape on the lower edge.

19. Cut the Drawer Support Panels to the size specified on the drawing.

20. Glue and clamp these panels to the edges of the Support Stretchers, as shown on the drawing.

21. Glue the edge of the remaining Drawer Support Panel and clamp it to the top inside edge of the Bottom Stretcher. (This forms a 90˚ angle.)

22. Dry assemble the Left Side Assembly and the Right Side Assembly with the Drawer Supports.

23. *Cut the decorative front edges on both Front Legs.* Use the lines on the photocopy as a guide. (The photocopy was attached in the first section of the construction sequence.)

24. Apply glue to the tenons, the ends of all Drawer Support Panels, and the mortises in the Front Legs. Clamp the assembly together, ensuring all Drawer Supports are aligned with the pencil marks and square with the Side Panel Assemblies.

Technical Note:
The Back Legs have a rabbet cut on the edge. The finished size of these pieces is ½" x ½". These finished pieces would be too small to handle safely when cutting the rabbet. Using a board of an oversized width improves the safety of this operation.

Technical Note:
Mark a pencil line on the inside of the Left Side Assembly and on the inside of the Right Side Assembly where the Drawer Supports should align. Use a square to ensure the line is square with the Side Assemblies. This line will be used during the glue-up process to ensure the Drawer Supports are square with the Side Panel Assemblies.

25. Cut the Back to the size specified on the materials list. Confirm that the width dimension specified on the materials list matches the Chest Assembly made in the previous steps. Alter it, if needed.

26. Apply glue to the rabbets in the Back Legs and along the back edge of the Drawer Supports. Clamp the Back to the Chest Assembly and make sure it is flush with the top ends of the Back Legs.

27. Cut the Chest Top to the size specified on the materials list.

28. Apply glue to the top surface of the top Drawer Support Panel and clamp the Chest Top to the Chest Assembly. Ensure the Chest Top is centered on the width of the Chest Assembly and flush with the Back.

Making the Drawers

29. Cut the Drawer Fronts to the sizes specified on the materials list.

30. Cut the rabbet on each Drawer Front as specified.

31. Cut the materials for the Drawer Sides, the Drawer Backs, and the Drawer Bottoms to the sizes specified on the materials list.

32. Glue and clamp the Drawer Sides, the Drawer Backs, and the Drawer Bottoms to the Drawer Fronts.

33. Mark the locations for the Wood Knobs and mount them. Inset the Wood Knobs 1" from each end and centered on the Drawer width.

Finishing

34. Sand the chest and apply a finish.

Technical Note:
Dry fit each Drawer Unit and test fit the Drawers into the Chest Assembly. Adjust the Drawer pieces before assembly. Use tape to temporarily hold the Drawer pieces together.

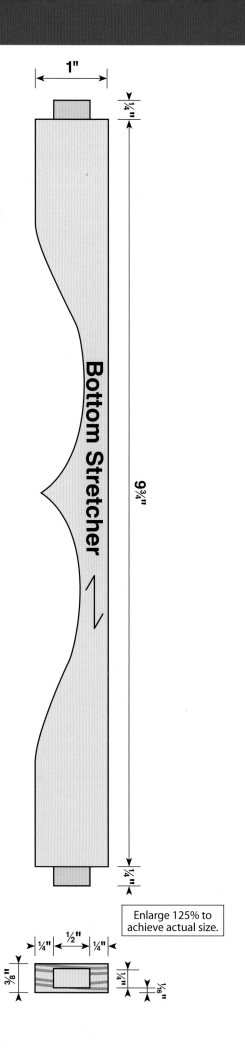

1"

¼"

Bottom Stretcher

9¾"

¼"

Enlarge 125% to achieve actual size.

¼" ½" ¼"

⅜" ¼" 1/16"

Side Panel Assembly

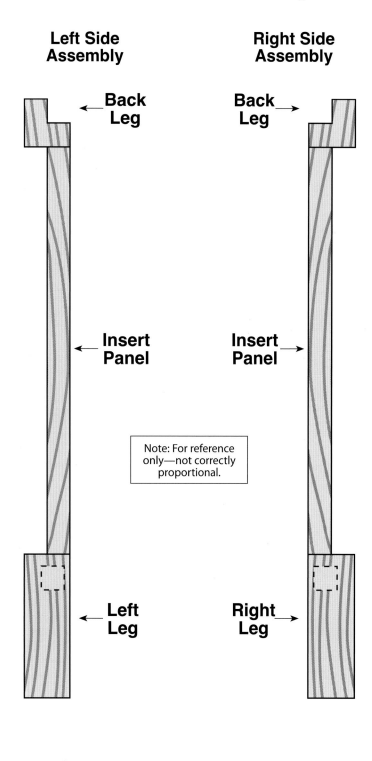

Left Side Assembly

Back Leg ←

Insert Panel ←

Note: For reference only—not correctly proportional.

Left Leg ←

Right Side Assembly

→ Back Leg

→ Insert Panel

→ Right Leg

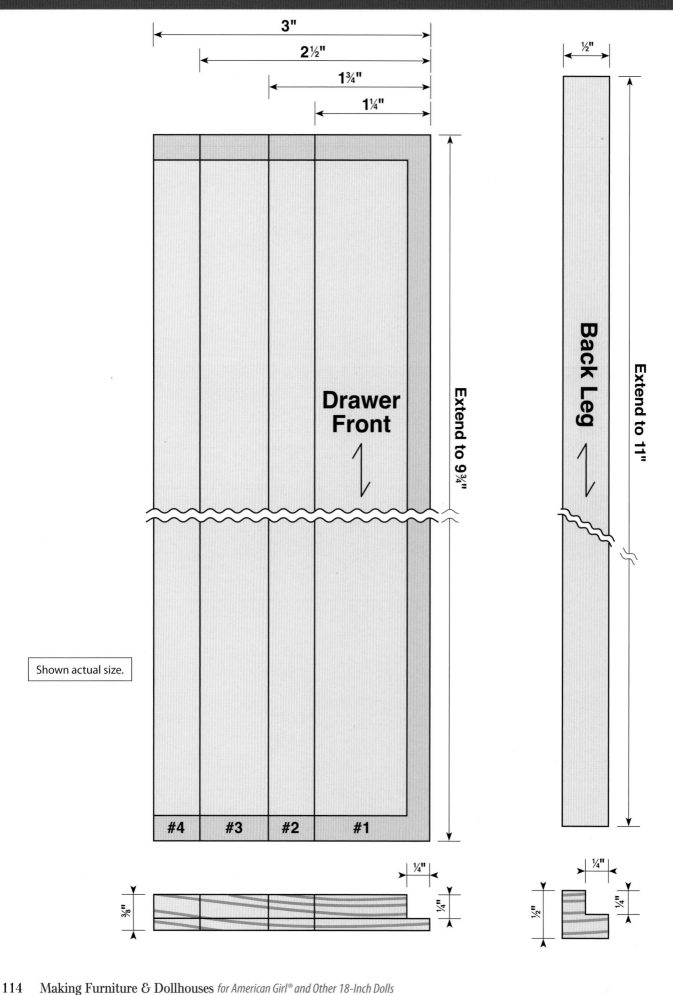

3"

2½"

1¾"

1¼"

Drawer Front

Extend to 9¾"

Back Leg

½"

Extend to 11"

Shown actual size.

#4   #3   #2   #1

3/8"   ¼"   ¼"

½"   ¼"   ¼"

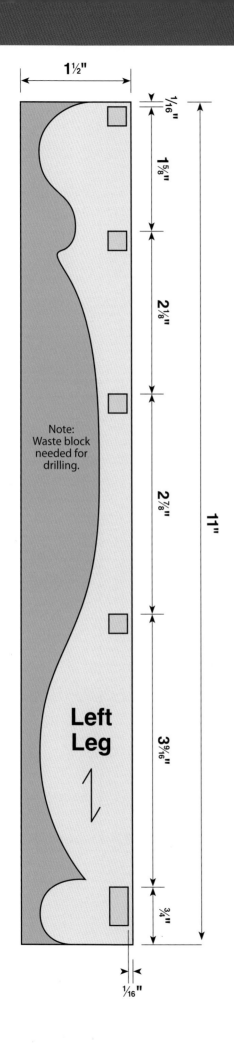

1½"

1/16"

1⅝"

2⅛"

2⅞"

11"

Note:
Waste block
needed for
drilling.

**Left
Leg**

3⁹/₁₆"

¾"

1/16"

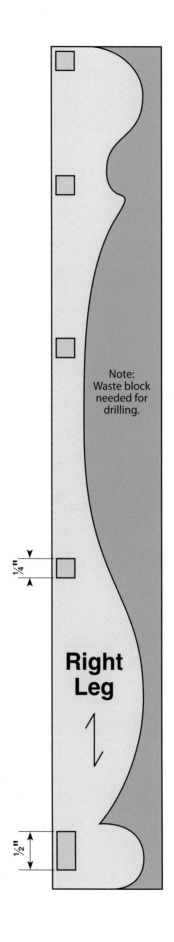

Note:
Waste block
needed for
drilling.

**Right
Leg**

¼"

½"

Enlarge 125% to
achieve actual size.

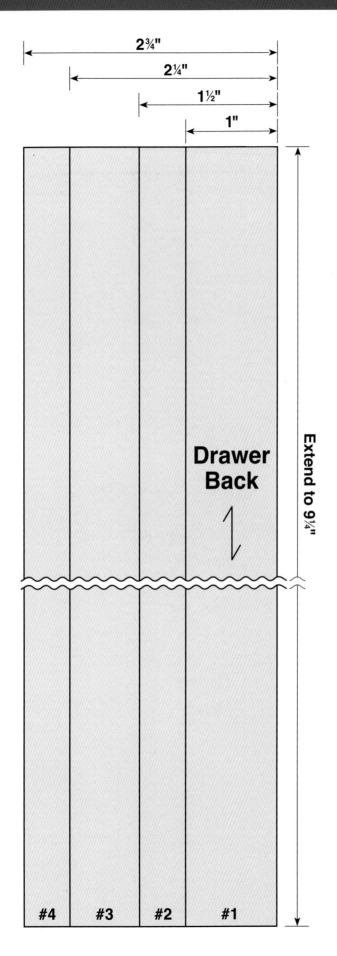

2¾"

2¼"

1½"

1"

**Drawer
Back**

Extend to 9¼"

#4 #3 #2 #1

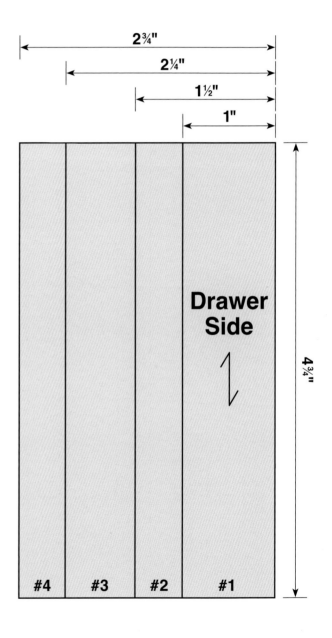

2¾"

2¼"

1½"

1"

**Drawer
Side**

4¾"

#4 #3 #2 #1

Shown actual size.

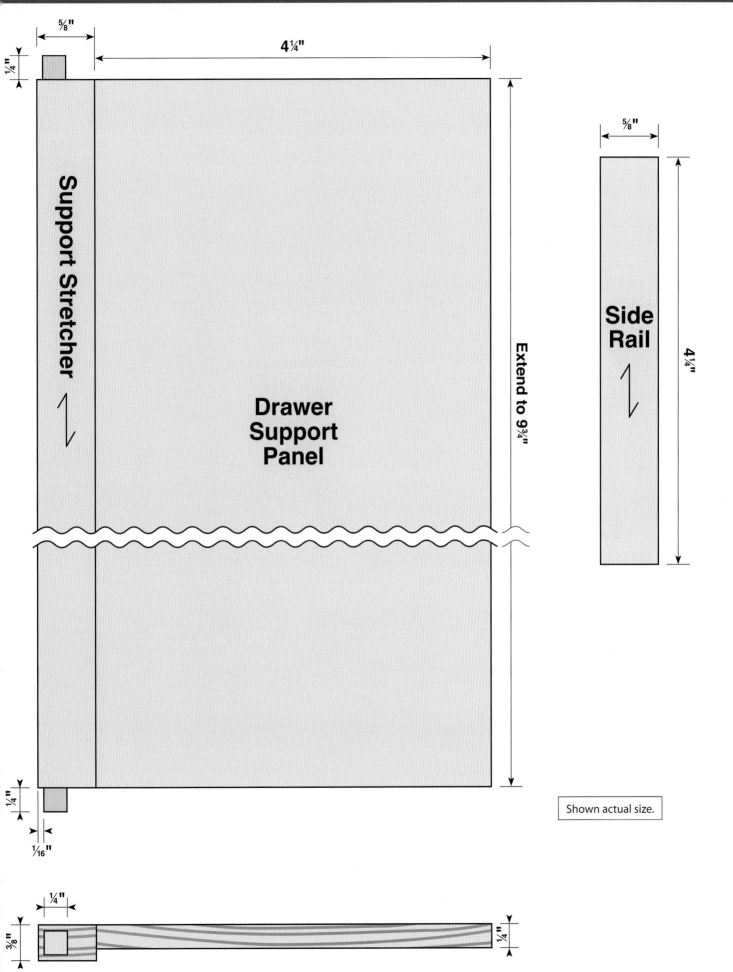

5/8"

1/4"

4¼"

Support Stretcher

Drawer Support Panel

Extend to 9¾"

1/4"

1/16"

1/4"

3/8"

1/4"

5/8"

Side Rail

4¼"

Shown actual size.

Short Dresser

Materials List

Item	Width	Length	Thickness	Quantity	Material	Location
Back	6¼" (159mm)	6⅝" (168mm)	¼" (6mm)	1	Walnut	No drawing
Back Leg	½" (13mm)	7" (178mm)	½" (13mm)	2	Walnut	Page 123
Bottom Stretcher	1" (25mm)	6¼" (159mm)	⅜" (10mm)	1	Walnut	Page 124
Chest Top	6" (152mm)	7¼" (184mm)	⅜" (10mm)	1	Walnut	No drawing
Drawer Back #1	1" (25mm)	5¼" (133mm)	¼" (6mm)	1	Plywood	Page 125
Drawer Back #2	1⅜" (35mm)	5¼" (133mm)	¼" (6mm)	1	Plywood	Page 125
Drawer Back #3	1¾" (44mm)	5¼" (133mm)	¼" (6mm)	1	Plywood	Page 125
Drawer Bottom	4¾" (121mm)	5¾" (146mm)	¼" (6mm)	3	Plywood	No drawing
Drawer Front #1	1¼" (32mm)	5¾" (146mm)	⅜" (10mm)	1	Walnut	Page 125
Drawer Front #2	1⅝" (41mm)	5¾" (146mm)	⅜" (10mm)	1	Walnut	Page 125
Drawer Front #3	2" (51mm)	5¾" (146mm)	⅜" (10mm)	1	Walnut	Page 125
Drawer Side #1	1" (25mm)	4¾" (121mm)	¼" (6mm)	2	Plywood	Page 125
Drawer Side #2	1⅜" (35mm)	4¾" (121mm)	¼" (6mm)	2	Plywood	Page 125
Drawer Side #3	1¾" (44mm)	4¾" (121mm)	¼" (6mm)	2	Plywood	Page 125
Drawer Support Panel	4¼" (108mm)	5¾" (146mm)	¼" (6mm)	4	Walnut	Page 123
Insert Panel	4¼" (108mm)	6" (152mm)	¼" (6mm)	2	Walnut	No drawing
Left Leg	1½" (38mm)	7" (178mm)	½" (13mm)	1	Walnut	Page 122
Right Leg	1½" (38mm)	7" (178mm)	½" (13mm)	1	Walnut	Page 122
Side Panel Assembly						Page 124
Side Rail	⅝" (16mm)	4¼" (108mm)	⅜" (10mm)	2	Walnut	No drawing
Support Stretcher	⅝" (16mm)	6¼" (159mm)	⅜" (10mm)	3	Walnut	Page 123
Wood Knob			⅝" (16mm) Dia.	6		No drawing

Making the Side Panel Assemblies

1. Select hardwood materials of the proper thickness for each chest part.

2. Cut the materials to the sizes specified on the drawings for the Left Leg and the Right Leg.

3. Photocopy the drawings for these Legs. Use temporary adhesive to attach the photocopy to the wood pieces.

4. Lay out the locations of the mortises as specified on the drawings for the Left Leg and the Right Leg pieces.

5. Use a ¼" mortise drill to cut all mortises ⅜" deep and to the length specified on the drawings. *Do not cut the decorative shape on the front edge of the Legs at this time.*

6. Cut a ½" board to 11" long and an oversized width (approximately 4" wide). This board will be used to make the Back Legs.

7. Cut a rabbet on both edges of the oversized board as specified on the drawing for the Back Legs.

Technical Note:
The Back Legs have a rabbet cut on the edge. The finished size of these pieces is ½" x ½". These finished sizes are too small to handle safely when cutting the rabbet. Using a board with an oversized width improves the safety of this operation.

8. Cut the Back Leg pieces from the oversized board to the width specified on the drawing.

9. Cut the Insert Panel pieces to the size specified on the drawing.

10. Cut the Side Rail pieces to the size specified on the drawing.

11. Apply glue to the end of the Insert Panel and clamp it to the Side Rail. Ensure the Side Rail is flush with the face of the Insert Panel.

12. Apply glue to the edge of the Insert Panel and clamp it to the Left Leg. Ensure the Insert Panel is flush with the side of the Front Leg with mortises and flush with the top end of the Front Leg.

13. Apply glue to the edge of the Insert Panel and clamp it to the Back Leg. Ensure the Insert Panel is flush with the inside and top of the Back Leg. Reference the Left Side Assembly drawing for proper orientation of the Back Leg.

14. Use the same procedure outlined above to assemble the Right Side Assembly.

Making the Chest Assembly

15. Cut the Support Stretcher and Bottom Stretcher pieces to the sizes specified on the drawings.

16. Lay out and cut the tenons on these pieces as specified on the drawings.

17. Dry fit the tenons into the mortises in the Left Side Assembly and the Right Side Assembly.

18. Photocopy the drawing for the Bottom Stretcher. Use temporary adhesive to attach the photocopied pattern to the Bottom Stretcher and cut out the decorative shape on the lower edge.

19. Cut the Drawer Support Panels to the size specified on the drawing.

20. Glue and clamp the Drawer Support Panels to the edge of the Support Stretcher, as shown in the drawing.

21. Glue the edge of the remaining Drawer Support Panel and clamp it to the Top inside edge of the Bottom Stretcher. (This forms a 90° angle.)

22. Dry assemble the Left Side Assembly and the Right Side Assembly with the Drawer Supports.

23. Cut the decorative front edges on both Front Legs. Use the lines on the photocopy as a guide. (The photocopy was attached in the first section of the construction sequence.)

24. Apply glue to the tenons, the ends of all Drawer Support Panels, and the mortises in the Front Legs. Clamp the assembly together, ensuring all Drawer Supports are aligned with the pencil marks and square with the Side Panel Assemblies.

25. Cut the Back to the size specified on the materials list. Confirm the width dimension specified on the materials list matches the Chest Assembly made in the previous steps.

Technical Note:
Mark a pencil line on the inside of the Left Side Assembly and on the inside of the Right Side Assembly where the Drawer Supports should align. Use a square to ensure that the line is square with the Side Assemblies. This line will be used during the glue-up process to ensure that the Drawer Supports are square with the Side Panel Assemblies.

26. Apply glue to the rabbets in the Back Legs and along the back edge of the Drawer Supports. Clamp the Back to the Chest Assembly and ensure it is flush with the top ends of the Back Legs.

27. Cut the Chest Top to the size specified on the materials list.

28. Apply glue to the top surface of the top Drawer Support Panel and clamp the Chest Top to the Chest Assembly. Ensure the Chest Top is centered on the width of the Chest Assembly and flush with the Back.

Making the Drawers

29. Cut the Drawer Fronts to the sizes specified on the drawings.

30. Cut the rabbet on each Drawer Front as specified on the drawings.

31. Cut the materials for the Drawer Sides, the Drawer Backs, and the Drawer Bottoms to the sizes specified on the drawings and the materials list.

32. Glue and clamp the Drawer Sides, the Drawer Backs, and the Drawer Bottoms to the Drawer Fronts.

33. Mark the locations of the Wood Knobs and mount them on the Drawers. Inset the Wood Knobs 1" from each end and centered on the Drawer width.

Technical Note:
Dry fit each Drawer Unit and test fit the Drawers into the Chest Assembly. Adjust the Drawer pieces before assembly. Use tape to temporarily hold the Drawer pieces together.

Finishing

34. Sand the chest and apply a finish.

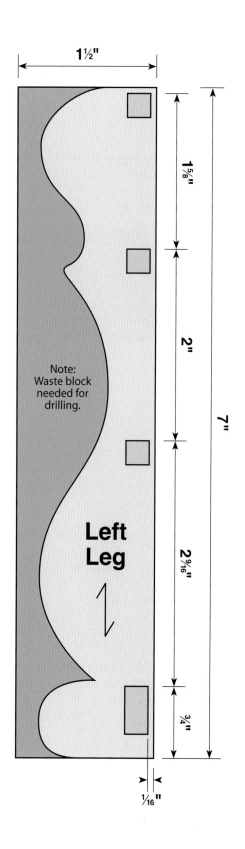

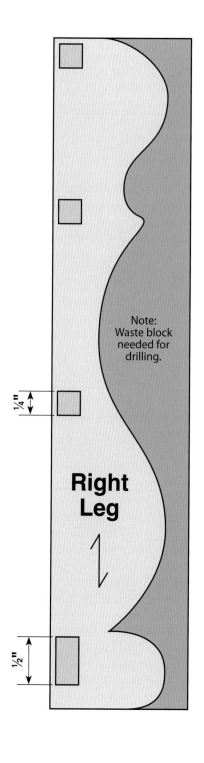

Shown actual size.

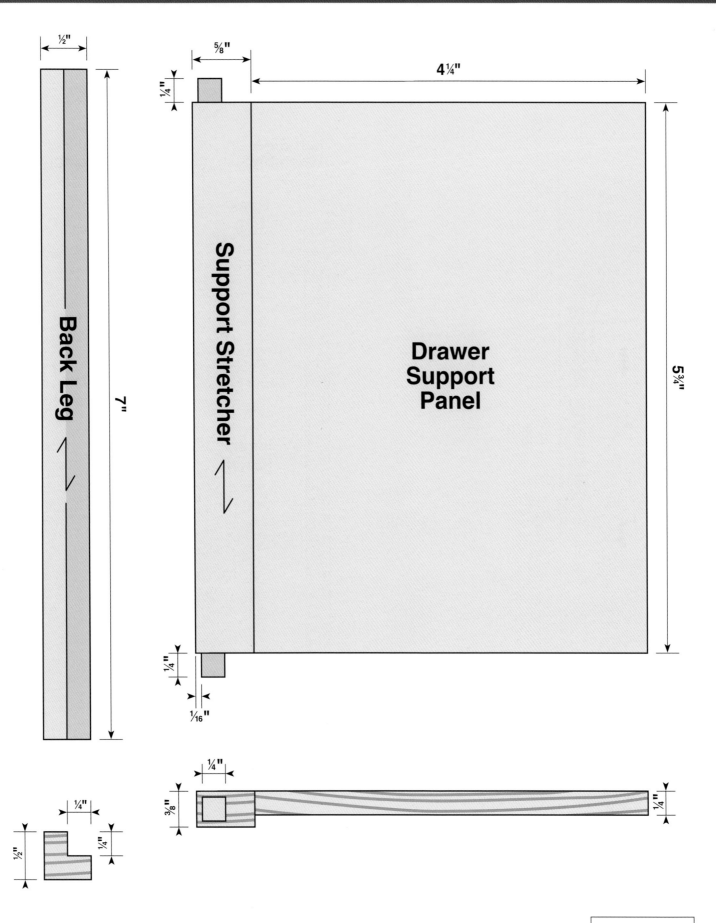

½"

5⁄8"

4¼"

¼"

Back Leg

7"

Support Stretcher

Drawer Support Panel

5¾"

¼"

1⁄16"

¼"

½"

¼"

3⁄8"

¼"

¼"

Shown actual size.

1"

¼"

Bottom Stretcher

5¾"

¼"

Shown actual size.

¼" ½" ¼"

⅜" ¼"

1/16"

Side Panel Assembly

**Left Side
Assembly**

**Right Side
Assembly**

Back
Leg ←

Back
Leg →

Insert
Panel ←

Insert
Panel →

Note: For reference
only—not correctly
proportional.

Left
Leg ←

Right
Leg →

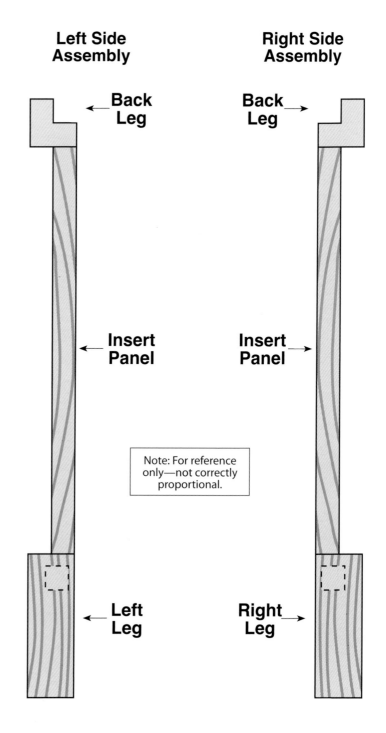

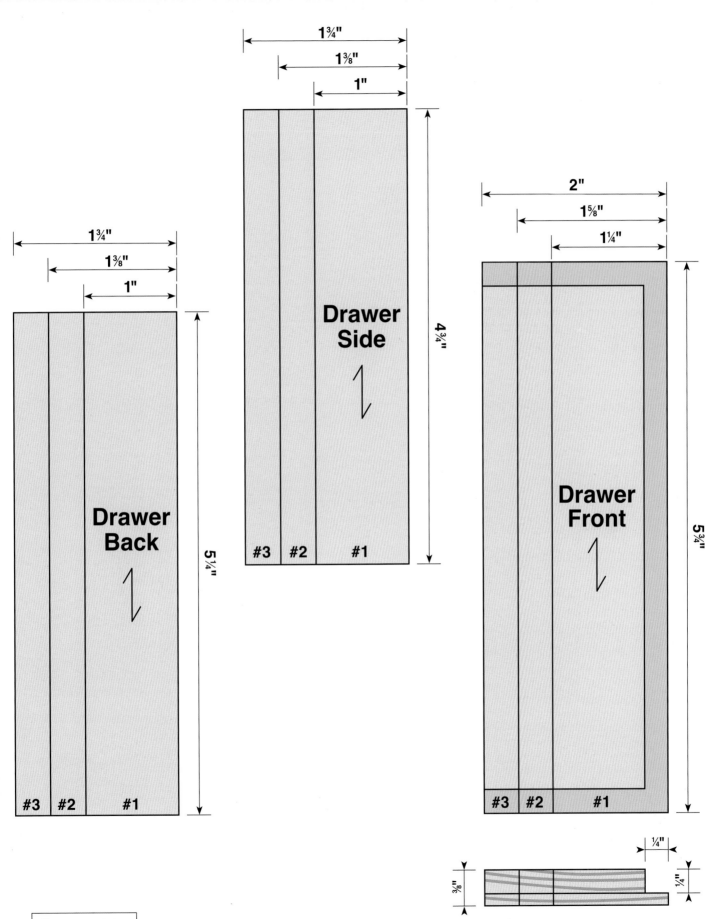

1¾"

1⅜"

1"

Drawer Side

4¾"

#3 #2 #1

1¾"

1⅜"

1"

Drawer Back

5¼"

#3 #2 #1

2"

1⅝"

1¼"

Drawer Front

5¾"

#3 #2 #1

¼"

¼"

⅜"

Shown actual size.

Armoire

Materials List

Item	Width	Length	Thickness	Quantity	Material	Location
Base Front & Back	1" (25mm)	11¼" (285mm)	⅜" (10mm)	1	Poplar	Page 133
Base Side	1" (25mm)	7⅞" (200mm)	⅜" (10mm)	2	Poplar	Page 133
Case Back	10½" (267mm)	17" (432mm)	¼" (6mm)	1	Poplar	No drawing
Case Bottom & Center Shelf	7" (178mm)	10" (254mm)	½" (13mm)	2	Poplar	Page 130
Case Side	7" (178mm)	17" (432mm)	½" (13mm)	2	Poplar	Page 132
Case Top End	6¾" (171mm)	10" (254mm)	¼" (6mm)	1	Poplar	No drawing
Door	4¹¹⁄₁₆" (119mm)	12¼" (311mm)	¼" (6mm)	2	Poplar	Page 131
Door & Drawer Front Trim	⅝" (16mm)	112" (2845mm)	⅛" (3mm)	1	Poplar	Page 131
Drawer Back	2⅞" (73mm)	9" (229mm)	¼" (6mm)	1	Plywood	No drawing
Drawer Bottom	6½" (165mm)	9" (229mm)	¼" (6mm)	1	Plywood	No drawing
Drawer Front	2⅞" (73mm)	9" (229mm)	¼" (6mm)	1	Poplar	Page 131
Drawer Side	2⅞" (73mm)	6½" (165mm)	¼" (6mm)	2	Plywood	No drawing
Hinge	½" (13mm)	⅝" (16mm)		4	Hardware	
Rod	¼" (6mm)	10" (254mm)		1	Dowel	No drawing
Rod Hanger	2" (51mm)	6½" (165mm)	⅜" (10mm)	2	Poplar	Page 134
Splat	2" (51mm)	10¾" (273mm)	½" (13mm)	1	Poplar	Page 133
Stile	¾" (19mm)	17" (432mm)	½" (13mm)	2	Poplar	Page 134
Top	7¾" (197mm)	11¼" (285mm)	¼" (6mm)	1	Poplar	No drawing
Top Rail	¾" (19mm)	9½" (241mm)	½" (13mm)	1	Poplar	Page 134
Wood Knob			⅝" (16mm) Dia.	2		

Assembling the Case

1. Select hardwood materials of the proper thickness for each part.
2. Cut the Case Sides to the width and length specified on the drawing.
3. Cut the rabbet on the edge of the Case Side materials as specified on the drawing.
4. Cut the Case Back to the width and length specified.
5. Apply glue to the rabbet on the Case Sides and clamp the Case Sides to the Case Back. Ensure the assembly is square.
6. Cut the Case Top End to the width and length specified.
7. Glue and clamp the Case Top End to the Case Assembly.
8. Cut a piece of ½"-thick wood, 4" wide and 27" long, to use in making the Stiles.
9. Cut a ¼" x ¼" rabbet on both edges of this board.
10. Cut the Stiles and the Top Rail pieces from the board to the widths and lengths specified on the drawings.
11. Apply glue to the rabbet groove on the Stiles and clamp them to the Case Sides.
12. Cut the material for the Case Bottom & Center Shelf pieces to the width and length specified on drawing.

Technical Note:
The Stile and the Top Rail pieces have a rabbet cut on the edge. The finished size of these pieces is ½" x ¼". These pieces would be too small to handle safely when cutting the rabbet. Using a wider board improves the safety of this operation.

13. Cut ¼" x ½" notches in the two front corners where these pieces will fit with the Stiles. The Case Bottom & Center Shelf pieces will fit inside the assembly and will be flush with the front face of the Stiles.

14. Glue and clamp the Case Bottom to the Case Sides and the Case Back. Ensure that the Case Bottom is flush with bottom edges of the Case Assembly.

15. Mark the location of the Center Shelf, which is 3" from the Case Bottom.

16. Glue and clamp the Center Shelf to the Case Assembly. Ensure that the Center Shelf is aligned with the marks.

17. Cut the Top to the size specified.

18. Use a file and block sander to round the edges of the Top.

19. Apply glue to the Case End and clamp the Top to the Case Assembly. Ensure the Top is centered on the width and length of the Case Assembly.

20. Cut Rod Hanger pieces to the size and shape specified on the drawing.

21. Drill ¼"-diameter holes in the Rod Hanger pieces.

22. Cut the Rod to a length of 10".

23. Glue and clamp the Rod and the Rod Hanger pieces to the inside of the Case Assembly.

24. Sand the Case Assembly to smooth out any imperfections caused during assembly.

Making the Doors and the Trim Pieces

25. Cut the material for the Doors to the width and length specified on the drawing.

26. Cut approximately 112" of ⅛"-thick x ⅝"-wide wood for the Door & Drawer Front Trim. **Note:** Technically, you only need 97¼", but this thin wood breaks easily, so you may need some extra.

27. Cut four Door Front Trim pieces 12¼" long.

28. Glue and clamp these Door Front Trim pieces to the edges of the two Doors.

29. Cut four Door Front Trim pieces for the tops and bottoms of the two Doors. Glue and clamp to the Doors.

30. Test fit the trimmed Doors into the Door opening. Trim their widths or lengths if necessary.

31. Mark the locations for the Wood Knobs and attach them. They should be centered on the length of the Door and centered on the width of the Door Front Trim piece.

32. Mark the locations for the Hinges. These are located 1" in from the ends of both Doors.

33. Lay out and cut a mortise one-half the thickness of the folded hinge on the Doors.

34. Drill pilot holes and attach the Hinges to the Doors using #2 flat head screws.

35. Using the Hinges on the Doors as a guide, mark the locations on the Stiles where the Hinge mortises will be cut.

36. Cut the Hinge mortises in each Stile to one-half the thickness of the folded Hinge.

37. Drill pilot holes and attach the Hinges to the Doors using #2 flat head screws.

Technical Note:
Cut two short spacers from 3"-wide wood. Place these spacers against the Case Bottom to help ensure the alignment of the Center Shelf.

Technical Note:
The Door Front Trim on this project could be cut from individual pieces of wood and applied to the Doors to look more authentic. A simpler method is to cut the Door Front Trim pieces from a single piece of wood and attach them to the Doors as a single unit.

Technical Note:
Photocopy the pattern for the Doors. Cut out the segment of the pattern for the top Door Front Trim piece. Use temporary adhesive to attach this pattern segment to a piece of scrap wood. Cut out the template and use it as a marking guide for the other Door Front Trim pieces.

Making the Drawers

38. Cut the material for the Drawer Side, the Drawer Back, the Drawer Front, and the Drawer Bottom pieces.

39. Glue and clamp the Drawer pieces to each other to create a square Drawer.

40. Test fit the Drawer into the opening. Trim the Drawer Front so it fits the opening you've constructed.

41. Cut the Drawer Front Trim pieces using the drawing as a guide. Glue and clamp the pieces to the drawer.

Making the Base

42. Cut the materials for the Base Front, the Back, and the Base Sides to the widths specified on the drawings.

43. Cut these pieces 2" longer than the drawings indicate.

44. Cut a 45° miter on the ends of each piece to fit these pieces around the Armoire Case Assembly.

45. Photocopy the drawing for the Base Front and the Base Side pieces. Use temporary adhesive to attach the photocopied pattern to these pieces and cut the decorative edges on these pieces.

46. Glue and clamp the Base Front, the Back, and the Base Side pieces to the Armoire Case Assembly.

Making the Splat

47. Photocopy the drawing for the Splat. Use temporary adhesive to attach the photocopy to an oversized board.

48. Cut the upper portion of the Splat. Leave the lower portion of the Splat attached to the oversized board.

49. Remove ⅛" from the thickness of the oversized board.

50. Cut the lower portion of the Splat from the oversized board.

51. Glue and clamp both parts of the Splat together. Ensure the lower section of the Splat is flush with the back of the upper portion. This will create a ⅛" reveal on the front side of the Splat.

52. Glue and clamp the Splat to the Top. Set the Splat ⅜" back from the front edge of the Top. Center it on the width.

Finishing

53. Sand the armoire and apply a finish.

54. This armoire would also look attractive made from walnut or cherry.

55. Miniature-sized stencils are available from arts and crafts stores.

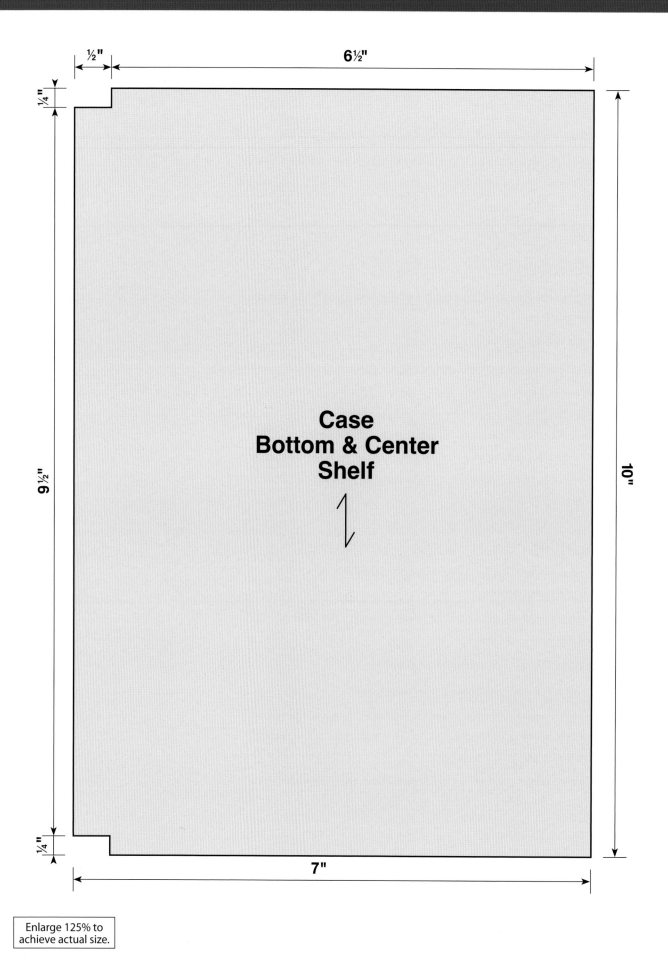

½"

6½"

¼"

9½"

Case
Bottom & Center
Shelf

10"

7"

Enlarge 125% to
achieve actual size.

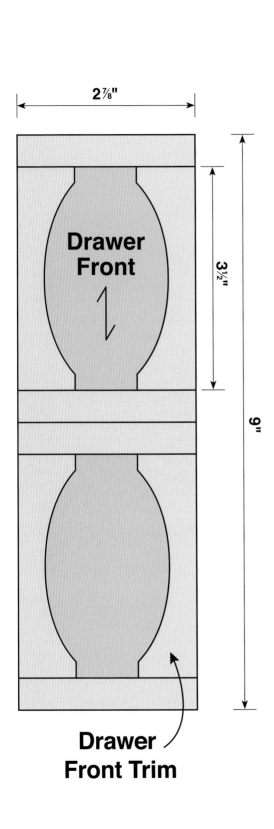

2⅞"

**Drawer
Front**

3½"

9"

**Drawer
Front Trim**

Enlarge 150% to
achieve actual size.

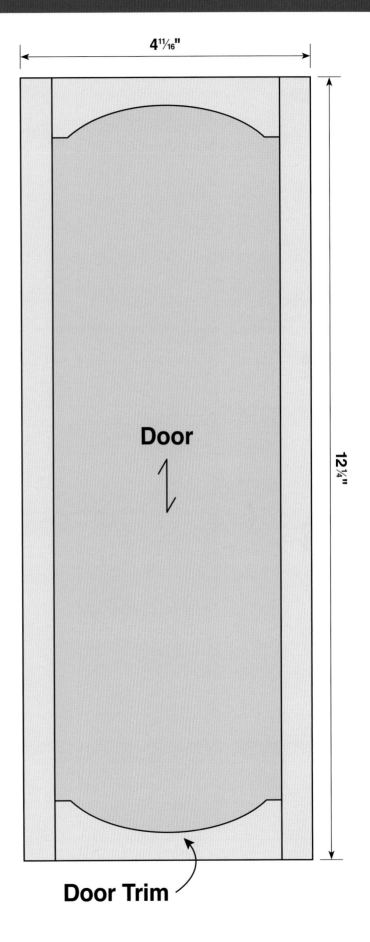

4¹¹⁄₁₆"

Door

12¼"

Door Trim

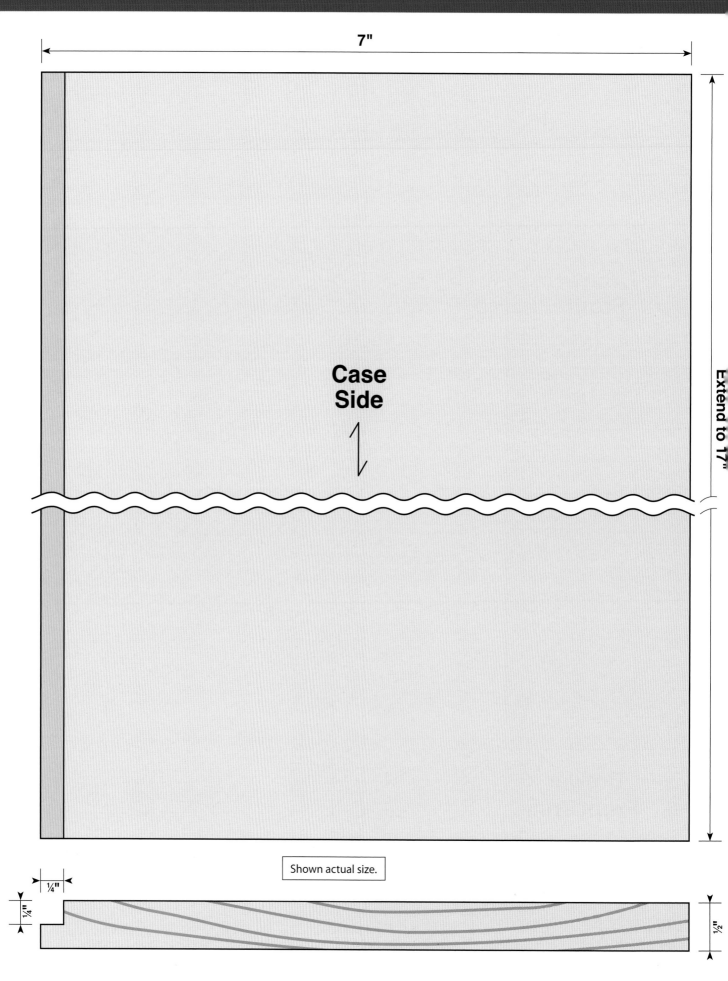

7"

Extend to 17"

**Case
Side**

Shown actual size.

¼"

¼"

½"

2"

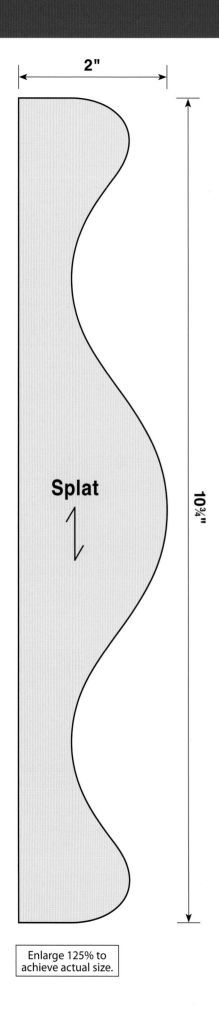

Splat

10¾"

1"

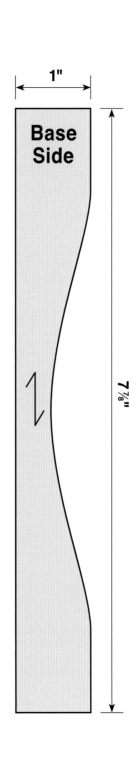

Base Side

7⅞"

1"

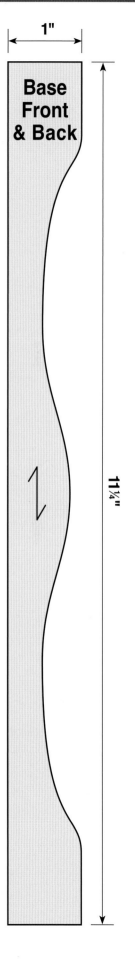

Base Front & Back

11¼"

Enlarge 125% to achieve actual size.

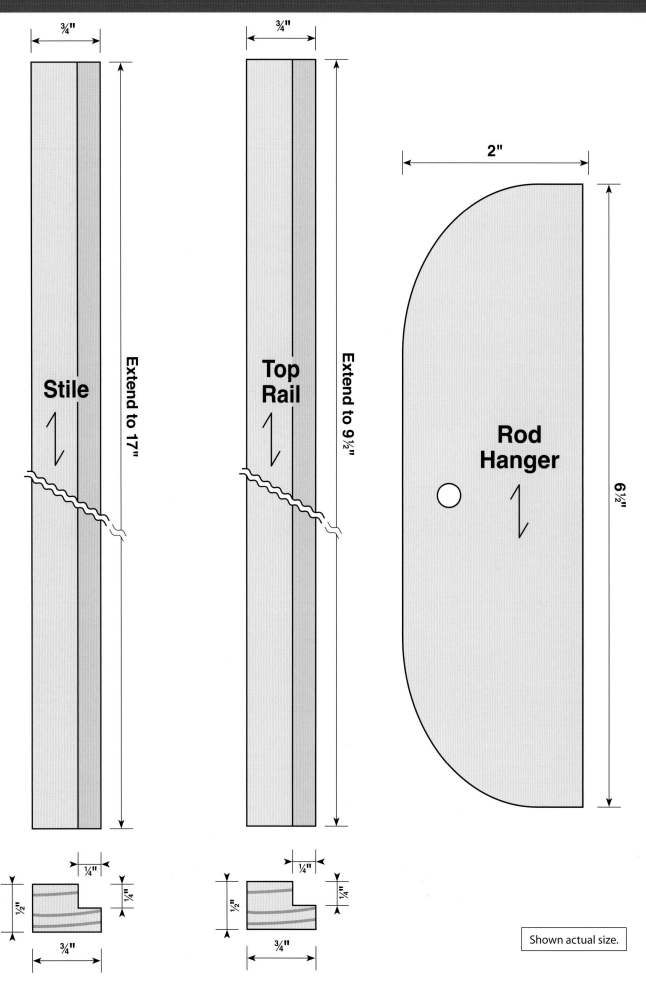

Stile

Extend to 17"

Top Rail

Extend to 9½"

2"

Rod Hanger

6½"

¾"

¾"

¼"

¼"

½"

½"

¼"

¼"

¾"

¾"

Shown actual size.

Treasure Chest

Materials List

Item	Width	Length	Thickness	Quantity	Material	Location
End	4¾" (121mm)	4¾" (121mm)	½" (13mm)	2	Bird's-eye	Page 137
Hasp		1⁵⁄₁₆" (33mm)		2	Brass Hardware	
Hinge	1" (25mm)	12" (305mm)		1	Piano Hardware	
Top, Bottom & Sides	4¾" (121mm)	12" (305mm)	½" (13mm)	4	Bird's-eye	Page 137

Making the Chest

1. Select hardwood materials of the proper thickness for each part on the materials list.

2. Cut a board to 4¾" width and 60" long.

3. Cut a 45° miter edge on both edges of the board.

4. Cut two pieces to 4¾" length for the Ends.

5. Cut four pieces to 12" length for the Top & Bottom and the Sides.

6. Cut a 45° miter on the ends of each piece.

7. Glue and clamp the Ends to the Sides. Ensure the assembly is square.

8. Glue and clamp the Top & Bottom to the Sides. This makes a totally enclosed box.

9. Cut the box to separate the lid from the remainder of the box. The lid thickness should be 1½".

10. Mark the location for the piano Hinge on the inside edges of the lid and the chest.

11. Cut the mortises in the lid and chest pieces to half the thickness of the folded Hinge.

12. Sand the chest and apply a finish.

13. Install the Hinge.

14. Mark the location and install the Hasp 2½" from the Ends.

15. The treasure chest could be made with surface mount hinges. This would eliminate the mortising step.

> **Technical Note:**
> The miters on this project were cut using a table router. The router bit depth was set so the router bit would not cut the full thickness of the board. This left an unmitered area ⅛" thick. This technique leaves a decorative effect at the edges. The miters may be cut to their full thickness to attain a sharp corner miter joint, if desired.

4¾"

12"

**Top,
Bottom
& Sides**

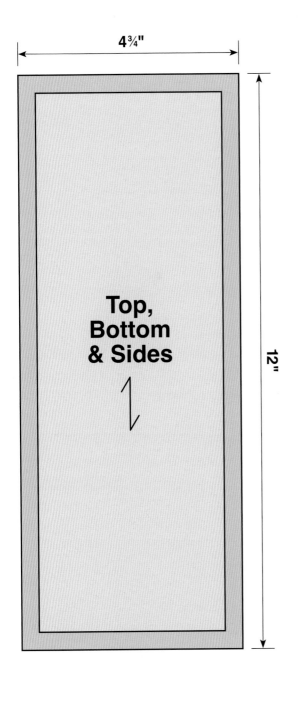

4¾"

4¾"

End

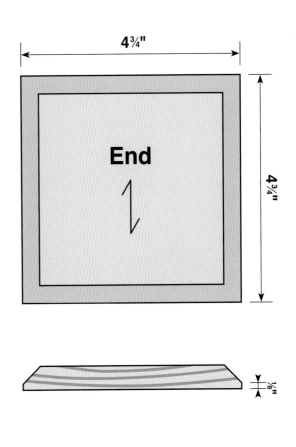

⅛"

⅛"

Enlarge 200% to
achieve actual size.

Page 139

Page 142

Page 151

Accessories

I n addition to chairs, tables, beds, and dressers, dolls need several other items to complete their surroundings. These items could conceivably include just about anything you see around you right now. For this book, I've zeroed in on four projects: the Bookcase, Grandfather Clock, Mirror, and School Desk. Any one of these items will help to complete a room scene.

The Bookcase, Grandfather Clock, and School Desk are made with simple box construction techniques learned in the chapter on dressers and chests. The Mirror requires the freehand use of a router on small wood pieces. The owner's manual and other training materials should be consulted to learn how to safely do this. The dimensional and decorative shapes in the oval mirror frame are made using a router. Cutting the rabbet groove in the mirror frame to the proper depth for the mirror's thickness is critical on this project. The mirror glass is easily cut from acrylic mirror sheet stock using a scroll saw.

Page 159

Bookcase

Materials List

Item	Width	Length	Thickness	Quantity	Material	Location
Back	6" (152mm)	8½" (216mm)	¼" (6mm)	1	Walnut	No drawing
Front	1" (25mm)	5½" (140mm)	⅜" (10mm)	1	Walnut	Page 141
Shelf	2¾" (70m)	5½" (140mm)	¼" (6mm)	4	Walnut	No drawing
Side	3" (76mm)	8½" (216mm)	⅜" (10mm)	2	Walnut	Page 141
Top	3¼" (83mm)	6⅝" (168mm)	⅜" (10mm)	1	Walnut	No drawing

Making the Sides and the Back

1. Select hardwood materials of the proper thickness for each bookcase part.

2. Cut a board 17" long and 3" wide for the Sides.

3. Cut a ¼" x ¼" rabbet on the edge of this board.

4. Cut the Side materials to the 8½" length specified on the drawing.

5. Cut the Back piece to the size specified on the materials list.

6. Apply glue to the rabbet groove in the Sides and assemble the Sides with the Back. Clamp the assembly until the glue is dry. Ensure that the assembly is square.

Making the Shelves

7. Cut the four Shelves to the length and width specified on the materials list.

8. Cut the Front piece to the size specified on the drawing.

9. Photocopy the pattern for the Front piece. Use temporary adhesive to attach the photocopy to the wood-piece for the Front and cut the decorative edge.

10. Apply glue to the top edge of the Front and clamp flush with the front edge of one of the Shelves.

11. Apply glue to three edges of the Bottom Shelf Assembly. Clamp this to the Bookcase Assembly.

12. Apply glue to all edges of the Top Shelf. Clamp flush with the top edge of the Bookcase Assembly. The Top Shelf is an end to the Shelf Assembly and a large surface for gluing the Top piece to the Bookcase Assembly.

13. Glue and clamp the Center Shelves to the Bookcase Assembly. Space the Upper Center Shelf 1½" down from the Top Shelf. Space the Lower Center Shelf 2½" up from the Bottom Shelf.

14. Sand the Bookcase Assembly to dress up any imperfections incurred during the assembly process.

> **Technical Note:**
> Use two short pieces of scrap wood, 1½" wide each, to align the Upper Center Shelf before clamping. Use two pieces of wood, 2½" wide each, as spacers for the Lower Center Shelf.

Making the Top

15. Cut the wood for the Top piece to the width and length specified on the materials list.

16. Glue and clamp the Top onto the Bookcase Assembly. Center the Top with the bookcase width and flush with the Back.

Finishing

17. Sand the bookcase and apply a finish.

3"

8½"

Side

1"

5½"

Front

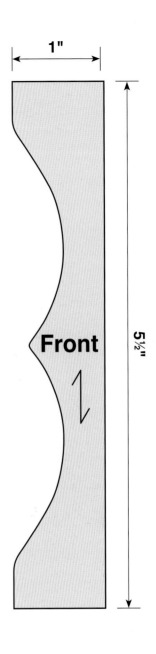

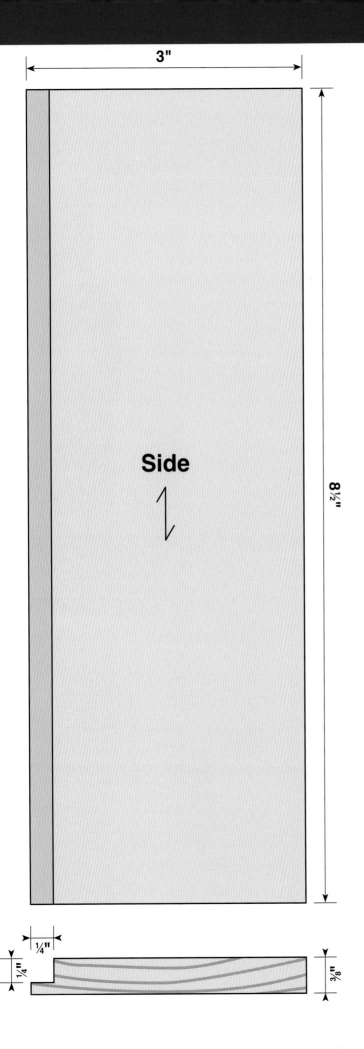

¼"

¼"

3"

⅜"

Shown actual size.

Grandfather Clock

Materials List

Item	Width	Length	Thickness	Quantity	Material	Location
BASE						
Clock Works			2¾" (70mm) Fit-up	1	Hardware	Check Klockit, (800) 556-2548, or Rockler, (800) 279-4441.
Front	1¾" (44mm)	5⅝" (143mm)	¾" (19mm)	1	Cherry	Page 146
Side	1¾" (44mm)	4" (102mm)	¾" (19mm)	2	Cherry	Page 147
Top	3½" (89mm)	5" (127mm)	¼" (6mm)	1	Walnut	Page 146
CENTER CASE						
Accent Door	3¹⁄₁₆" (78mm)	10½" (267mm)	⅛" (3mm)	1	Cherry	No drawing
Back	4⅛" (105mm)	12" (305mm)	¼" (6mm)	1	Walnut	No drawing
Door	4⅜" (111mm)	11⅞" (302mm)	¼" (6mm)	1	Walnut	No drawing
End	2¾" (70mm)	3⅝" (86mm)	¼" (6mm)	2	Walnut	No drawing
Hinge	½" (13mm)	⅝" (16mm)		2	Hardware	No drawing
Side	3" (76mm)	12" (305mm)	⅜" (10mm)	2	Walnut	Page 150
Wood Knob			⅝" (16mm) Dia.	1		No drawing
TOP CASE						
Back	5¼" (133mm)	5½" (140mm)	¼" (6mm)	1	Walnut	No drawing
Decorative Carving	1¼" (32mm)	5⅜" (137mm)		1		Check Meisel Hardware, (800) 441-9870, part #5954
Front	5½" (140mm)	5½" (140mm)	¼" (6mm)	1	Walnut	Page 149
Front Accent	4½" (114mm)	4½" (114mm)	⅛" (3mm)	1	Cherry	Page 148
Side	3" (76mm)	5½" (140mm)	⅜" (10mm)	2	Walnut	Page 148
Splat	1½" (38mm)	6" (152mm)	⅜" (10mm)	1	Walnut	Page 149
Top & Bottom	3¾" (76mm)	6" (152mm)	¼" (6mm)	2	Walnut	No drawing

Assembling the Top Case

1. Select hardwood materials of the proper thickness for each clock part.

2. Cut the Side material to the width and length specified on drawing.

3. Cut a ¼" x ¼" rabbet on the edge of the material for the Sides.

4. Cut the material for the Back to the width and length specified on the drawing.

5. Apply glue to the rabbet groove on the Sides. Assemble the Sides with the Back and clamp them together until the glue is dry. Ensure that the assembly is square.

6. Cut the material for the Front to the size specified on the drawing.

7. Lay out and cut the clock's 2⅜"-diameter hole in the center of the Front. The hole can be cut on a scroll saw or by using a Fostner bit in a drill press.

8. Apply glue to the front edges of the Sides and clamp the Front to the assembly.

9. Sand the assembly to dress up any imperfections that occurred during the assembly.

10. Photocopy the pattern for the Accent Front. Use temporary adhesive and attach the photocopied pattern to the wood piece selected for the Accent Front. Cut the Accent Front, following the pattern lines, and cut the 2⅜" clock hole.

11. Glue and clamp the Accent Front to the Front.

12. Cut the Top & Bottom to the size specified on the drawing.

13. Using a file and block sander, round over the front length and the two sides of the Top & Bottom pieces.

14. Apply glue to the top edge of the Top Case Assembly. Glue and clamp the Top to the assembly. Use the same procedure to attach the Bottom to the assembly. Center the Top & Bottom on the width of the assembly and make sure it is flush with the Back.

15. Photocopy the Splat pattern. Use temporary adhesive to attach the photocopy to the Splat and cut this piece.

16. Glue and clamp the Decorative Carving to the Splat.

17. Glue the Splat to the top of the assembly. Center it on the length of the Top, set back ⅜" from the rounded front edge.

Technical Note:
Actual Decorative Carving size may vary if purchased. Trim as desired.

Assembling the Center Case

18. Cut the Side material to the width and length specified on the drawing.

19. Cut a ¼" x ¼" rabbet on the edge of the material for the Sides.

20. Cut the material for the Back to the width and length specified on the drawing.

21. Apply glue to the rabbet groove on the Sides. Assemble the Sides with the Back and clamp these parts until the glue is dry. Ensure that the assembly is square.

22. Cut the Ends for the Center Case Assembly.

23. Glue and clamp the Ends to the assembly.

24. Sand the Center Case Assembly to dress up any imperfections from the assembly process.

25. Cut the materials for the Door and the Accent Door to the sizes specified on the materials list.

26. Glue and clamp the Accent Door to the Door. Center the Accent Door on the Door.

27. Lay out the locations for the Hinges 1½" from the ends of the Door.

28. Drill the Hinge holes and attach the Hinges to the Door using flathead screws.

29. Mark the location of the Hinges on the Center Case Assembly using the Door as a guide.

30. Cut a mortise into the side panel of the Center Case Assembly equal to the thickness of the folded Hinge. These Hinge mortises can be cut using a fret saw and a wood chisel.

31. Drill the Hinge hole location to attach the Door Assembly to the Center Case Assembly. Do not install the Door at this time.

32. Drill the hole in the Door for the Wood Knob. Glue and clamp the Knob to the Door.

33. Glue and clamp the Center Case Assembly to the Top Case Assembly. Ensure the Center Case Assembly is centered on the width of the Top Case Assembly and that the Backs are flush.

Assembling the Base

34. Cut a ¾"-thick board to the width specified on the drawing for the Front and Sides. The length of the board should be approximately 20". Do not cut this board into shorter pieces at this time.

35. Cut a ⅜" x ¼" rabbet on the edge of the 20"-long board.

36. Use a router with a ¼" radius cove bit to cut the edge opposite the rabbet on the 20"-long board.

37. Cut a 45° miter on each end of the Front piece for the base. The length specified on the drawing is approximate.

38. Cut a 45° miter on one end and cut to the length specified on the drawing for the left and right Sides.

39. Dry assemble the Front piece with the Sides. Measure the inside area of the rabbets where the Top piece will fit to determine the final size for the Top piece.

40. Cut the base Top to the size indicated on the drawing (adjusting the dimensions according to the measurements in the previous step).

41. Photocopy the pattern for the Front. Use a temporary adhesive to attach the photocopy to the Front. Cut the decorative shape on the bottom of the Front piece.

42. Apply glue to the miter corners and rabbet. Assemble the Sides, the Front, and the Top pieces and clamp the assembly.

43. Cut a piece of wood to fill in the back of the Base Assembly. Glue and clamp the filler piece flush with the back edge of the Base Assembly.

44. Sand the Base Assembly to dress up any imperfections from the assembly process.

45. Glue and clamp the Base Assembly to the Center Case Assembly. Ensure the Center Case Assembly is centered on the width of the Base Assembly and the Backs are flush.

Final Assembly and Finishing

46. Install the Door onto the Center Case Assembly using flathead screws to attach the Hinges.

47. Test the Door movement and adjust the length, if necessary.

48. Sand the clock and apply a finish.

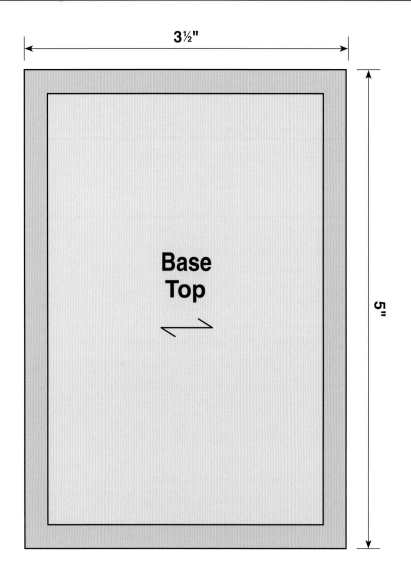

3½"

Base Top

5"

Shown actual size.

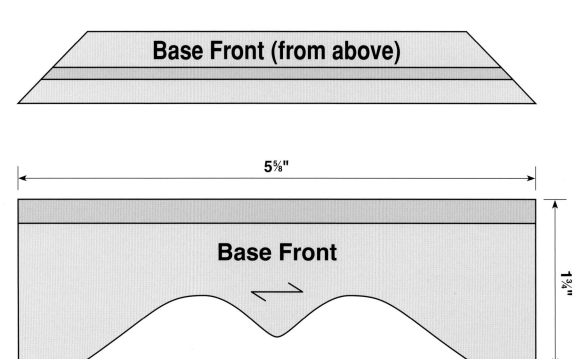

Base Front (from above)

5⅝"

Base Front

1¾"

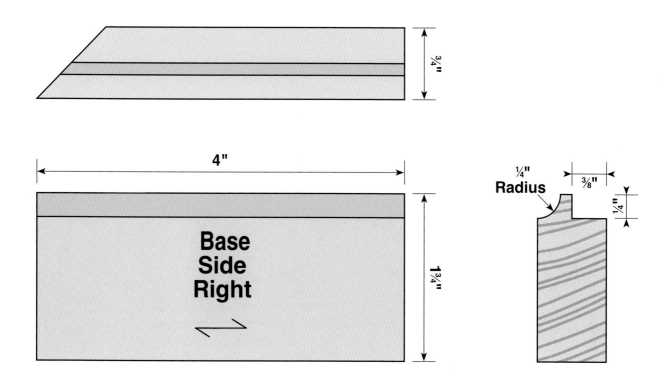

4"

**Base
Side
Right**

1¾"

¼"
Radius

⅜"

¼"

Shown actual size.

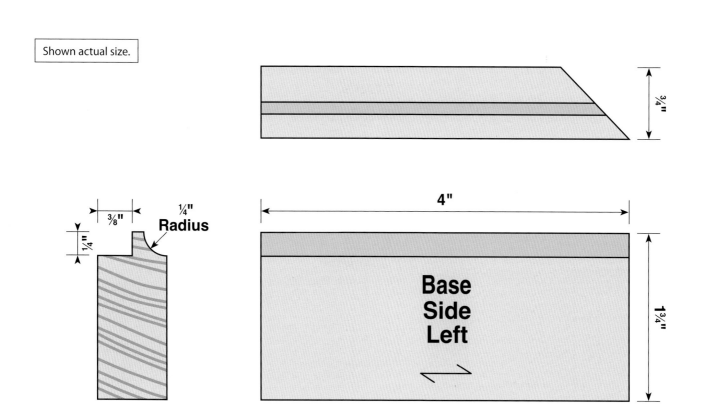

¾"

⅜"

¼"

¼"
Radius

4"

**Base
Side
Left**

1¾"

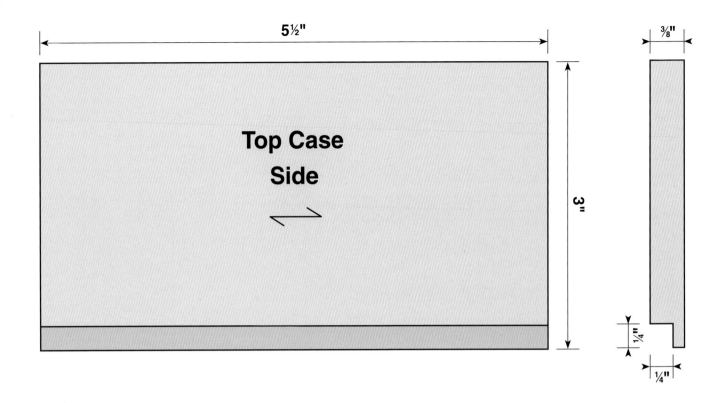

5½"

Top Case
Side

3"

³⁄₈"

¼"

¼"

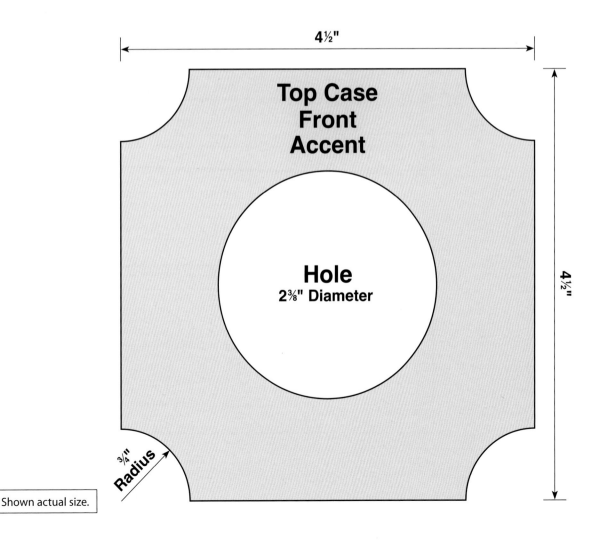

4½"

Top Case
Front
Accent

Hole
2³⁄₈" Diameter

4½"

³⁄₄"
Radius

Shown actual size.

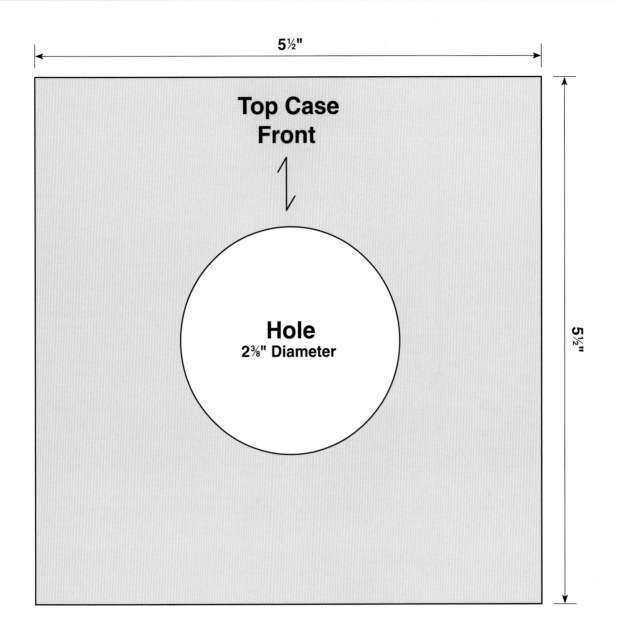

5½"

5½"

**Top Case
Front**

Hole
2⅜" Diameter

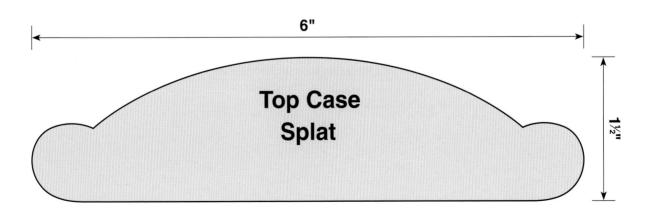

6"

1½"

**Top Case
Splat**

Shown actual size.

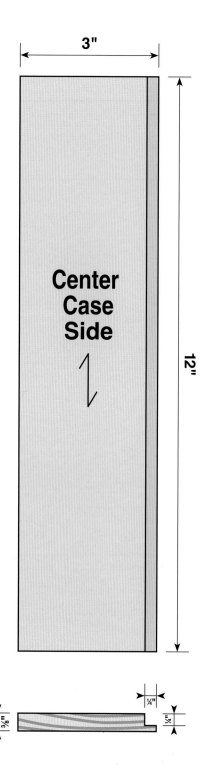

3"

Center
Case
Side

12"

3⁄8"

1⁄4"

1⁄4"

Enlarge 200% to
achieve actual size.

Mirror

Materials List

Item	Width	Length	Thickness	Quantity	Material	Location
Acrylic Mirror	5" (127mm)	9½" (241mm)	⅛" (3mm)	1	Acrylic	Page 154
Back Cover	5½" (140mm)	10" (254mm)	⅛" (3mm)	1	Plywood	Page 155
Decorative Carving	3¼" (83mm)	1½" (38mm)		1	Wood	Check Meisel Hardware, (800) 441-9870, part #5953
Foot	1⅞" (48mm)	6" (152mm)	¾" (19mm)	2	Walnut	Page 156
Frame	6" (152mm)	10½" (267mm)	¾" (19mm)	1	Cherry	Page 157
Leg	½" (13mm)	11½" (292mm)	½" (13mm)	2	Walnut	Page 156
Roundhead Screw		1¼" (32mm)	#6	2	Hardware	No drawing
Stretcher	2½" (64mm)	7" (178mm)	⅜" (10mm)	1	Walnut	Page 158

Making the Mirror

1. Select hardwood materials of the proper thickness for each part on the materials list.

2. Photocopy the drawing for the Frame piece. Attach the photocopy to an oversized piece of wood (6½" x 12") for the Frame.

3. Cut out the center hole in the Frame.

4. Sand the surfaces of the center hole to smooth out any imperfections from the saw blade.

5. Use a router with a pilot-guided rabbet bit to cut the ⅛"-deep rabbet around the center hole.

6. Use a router with a pilot-guided ⅜" cove bit to cut the decorative cove groove on the front side of the Frame.

7. Cut the outside dimensions of the Frame, following the lines on the photocopy.

8. Sand the outside surfaces to smooth out any imperfections from the saw blade.

9. Use a router with a pilot-guided ⅜" cove bit to cut the decorative groove on the outside of the Frame.

10. Photocopy the drawing for the Acrylic Mirror. Use temporary adhesive to attach the photocopy to the Acrylic Mirror. Cut the Mirror, following the lines on the photocopy.

11. Test fit the Acrylic Mirror in the Frame. Adjust the size, if necessary. Set the Acrylic Mirror in a safe place; it will be installed later in the sequence of construction.

12. Photocopy the drawing for the Back Cover. Use temporary adhesive to attach the photocopy to the ⅛" plywood and cut out the Back Cover.

13. Cut the pieces for the Leg, the Foot, and the Stretcher pieces.

14. Lay out and cut the tenons on the ends of the Stretcher and the two Leg pieces as specified on the drawings.

15. Lay out the mortise locations in the two Leg pieces, following the dimensions on the drawing.

16. Use a ¼" mortise bit to drill the mortise holes ¼" deep in the Leg pieces.

17. Use a file or a sanding block to make the decorative top on the Leg pieces. This is a 22° angle cut on four sides.

18. Lay out and drill clearance holes for the #6 Roundhead Screws that will serve as the support for the Frame.

19. Lay out mortises in the two Foot pieces. Use a ¼" mortise bit to drill the mortises ⅜" deep.

20. Dry fit the tenon on each Leg to the mortises in the Foot pieces.

21. Dry fit the tenons on the Stretcher with the mortises in the Leg pieces.

22. Drill screw pilot holes for the #6 Roundhead Screws in the Frame side. The holes should be centered on the height and thickness of the Frame.

23. Test fit the Frame into the Leg Support Assembly.

24. Disassemble all of the pieces.

25. Apply wood glue to the tenons on the Leg pieces and the mortises in the Foot pieces. Assemble and clamp until dry.

26. Apply wood glue to the Decorative Carving and clamp it to the Stretcher. Ensure the Decorative Carving is centered on the Stretcher.

27. Glue the tenons on the Stretcher to mortises in the Leg pieces. Clamp. Ensure the assembly is square.

28. Sand all the surfaces and apply a finish to the front and the sides of the Frame piece. Do not put any finish on the backside of the mirror Frame at this time.

29. Apply a finish to the Leg Support Assembly.

30. When all the coats of finish have dried, install the Acrylic Mirror and Back Cover.

31. Remove the protective vinyl sheet from the Acrylic Mirror. Place the Acrylic Mirror in the Frame.

32. Apply glue and clamp the Back Cover to the Frame. Ensure the Back Cover is centered on the Frame.

33. Apply a finish to the Back Cover and to the back of the Frame. Ensure no finish gets on the Acrylic Mirror because it may damage the acrylic plastic surface.

34. Mount the Frame Assembly in the Leg Support Assembly using two #6 Roundhead Screws.

Technical Note:
Actual Decorative Carving size may vary if purchased. Trim as desired.

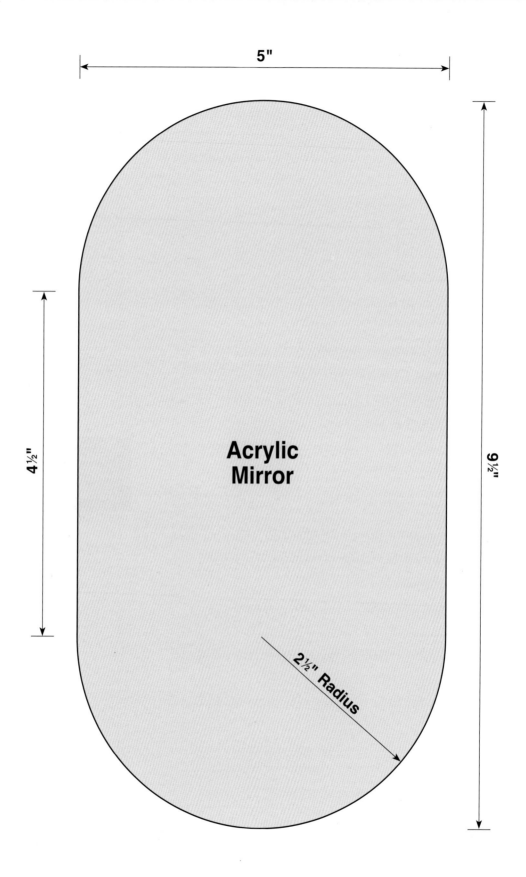

5"

9½"

4½"

**Acrylic
Mirror**

2½" Radius

Enlarge 125% to
achieve actual size.

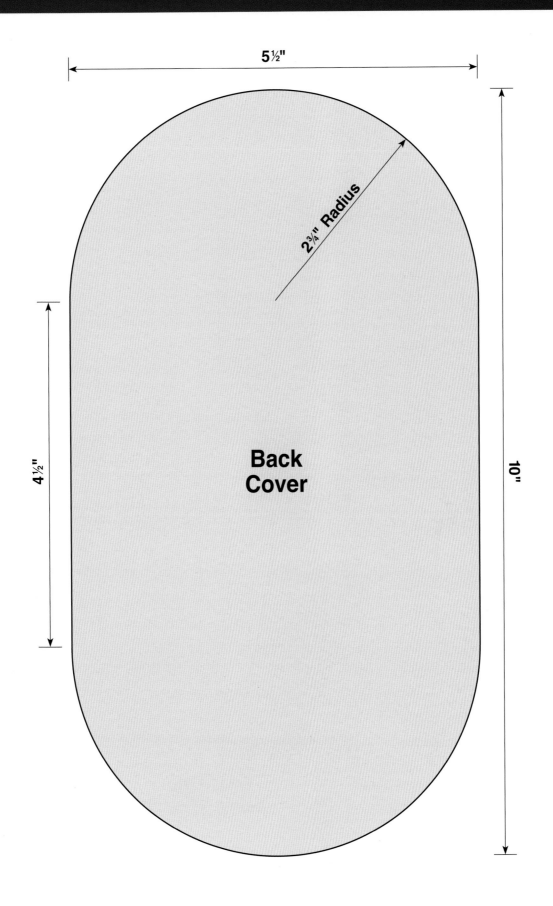

5½"

2¾" Radius

Back
Cover

4½"

10"

Enlarge 125% to
achieve actual size.

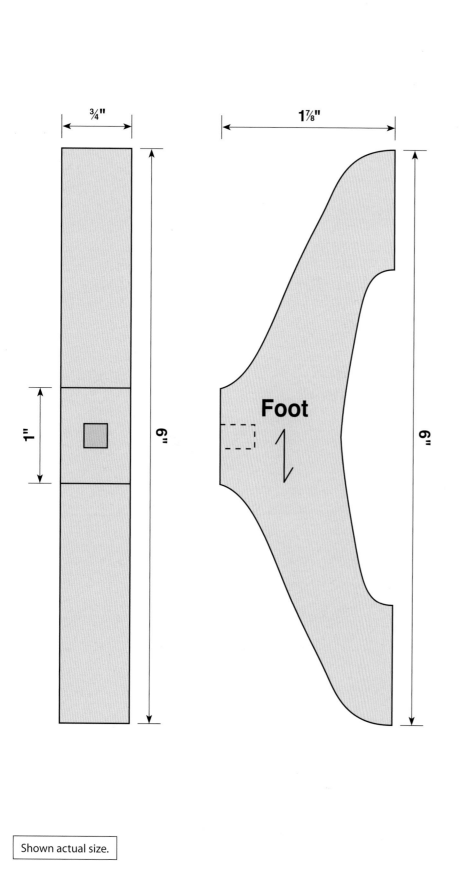

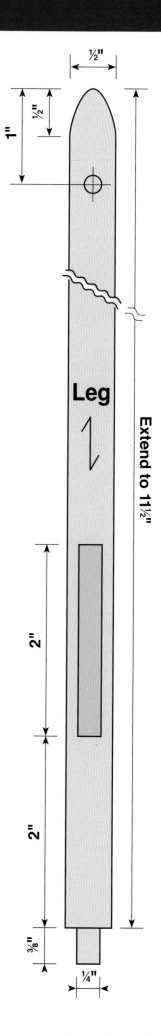

Foot

Leg

Shown actual size.

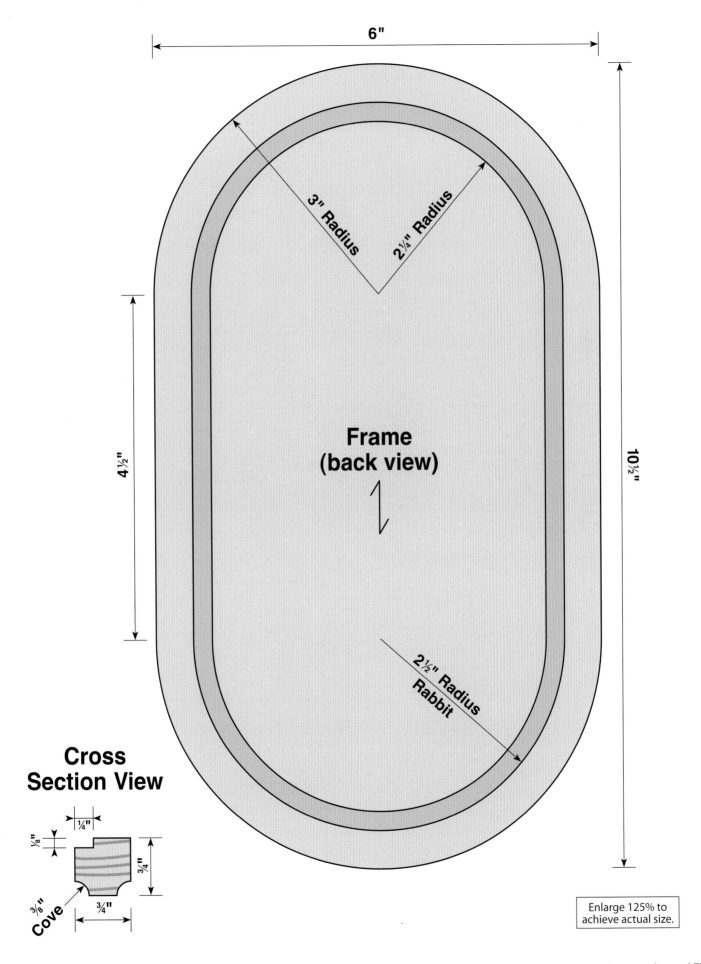

6"

3" Radius

2¼" Radius

4½"

10½"

**Frame
(back view)**

2½" Radius
Rabbit

**Cross
Section View**

¼"

⅛"

¾"

⅜"
Cove

¾"

Enlarge 125% to
achieve actual size.

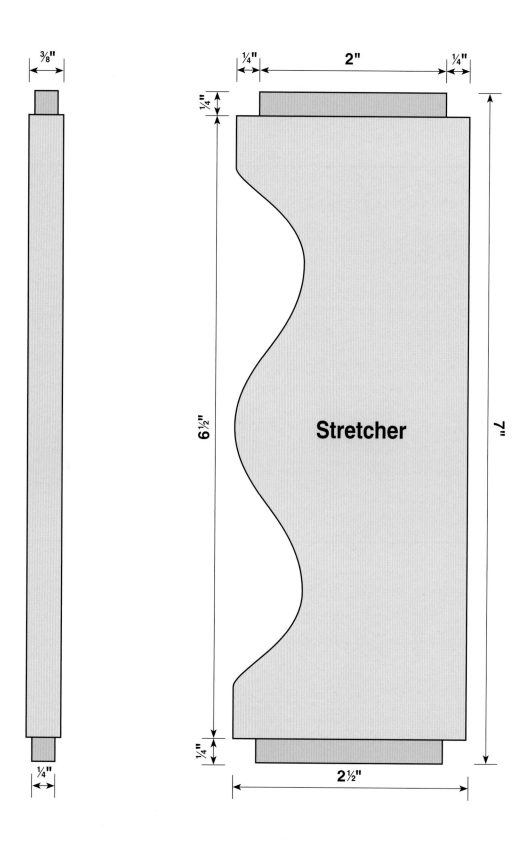

3/8"

1/4"

1/4"   2"   1/4"

1/4"

6 1/2"

7"

Stretcher

1/4"

2 1/2"

Shown actual size.

School Desk

Materials List

Item	Width	Length	Thickness	Quantity	Material	Location
Desk Case Back	2¼" (57mm)	6" (152mm)	⅜" (10mm)	1	Poplar	No drawing
Desk Case Floor	6" (152mm)	7" (178mm)	⅜" (10mm)	1	Poplar	No drawing
Desk Case Front	1⅛" (29mm)	6" (152mm)	⅜" (10mm)	1	Poplar	No drawing
Desk Case Side	2¼" (57mm)	5⅜" (137mm)	⅜" (10mm)	2	Poplar	Page 163
Desk Leg	5½" (140mm)	5½" (140mm)	½" (13mm)	2	Poplar	Page 164
Desk Top Narrow	1⅞" (48mm)	7" (178mm)	⅜" (10mm)	1	Poplar	Page 163
Desk Top Wide	4⅛" (105mm)	7" (178mm)	⅜" (10mm)	1	Poplar	Page 165
Hinge	½" (13mm)	⅝" (16mm)		2	Hardware	No drawing
Seat	4½" (114mm)	5½" (140mm)	⅜" (10mm)	1	Poplar	No drawing
Seat Back	4" (102mm)	5½" (140mm)	⅜" (10mm)	1	Poplar	No drawing
Seat Side	5½" (140mm)	8⅝" (219mm)	½" (13mm)	2	Poplar	Page 162
Support Stretcher	2½" (64mm)	5½" (140mm)	½" (13mm)	2	Poplar	Page 164

Cutting

1. Select hardwood materials of the proper thickness for each part on the materials list.

2. Photocopy the patterns for the Desk Legs, the Support Stretchers, and the Seat Sides.

3. Use temporary adhesive to attach the photocopies to the wood pieces selected for these parts.

4. Drill saw blade pilot holes for all the inside cuts on the Desk Leg, the Support Stretcher, and the Seat Side parts.

5. Cut out all these pieces using a scroll saw.

6. Rough-sand all the pieces to remove any saw marks and wood burrs.

Assembling the Desk Case

7. Lay out and cut all the pieces to the sizes specified on the drawings for the Desk Case Sides, the Desk Case Front, the Desk Case Back, the Desk Top Wide, the Desk Top Narrow, and the Desk Case Floor.

8. Cut a 16° angle on one edge of the Desk Top Wide, as specified on the drawing.

9. Lay out the location for the Hinges on the Desk Top Wide and the Desk Top Narrow pieces. The Hinges are located ½" in from the ends as shown on the drawing. Cut a mortise groove on both Top pieces. The mortise is the length of the Hinge and half the thickness of the folded Hinge.

10. Mark the Hinge hole locations and drill pilot holes. Install the Hinges to join both Top pieces using #2 flathead wood screws.

11. Round over the edges of the Desk Top Assembly and the Desk Case Floor. Use a file and sanding block to round over the edges. Do not round over the edges with the Hinges.

Technical Note:
If a micro-sized pilot twist drill is not available, use a small brad nail as a substitute.

12. Glue and clamp the Desk Case Sides to the Desk Case Front and the Desk Case Back pieces. Ensure the assembly is square.

13. Apply glue to the bottom edges of the Desk Case Assembly and clamp it to the Desk Case Floor. Center the Desk Case Floor on the Desk Case Assembly.

14. Glue and clamp the Desk Top Narrow piece to the Desk Case Assembly. Be sure the Hinge edge of the Desk Top Narrow is aligned with the point where the Desk Case Sides begin to slope.

15. Sand the Desk Case Assembly.

16. Glue and clamp one of the Support Stretchers between two of the Desk Legs. The glue point is noted on the drawing of the Desk Legs. Ensure the top edge of the Support Stretcher is flush with the top edges of the Desk Legs and that the assembly is square.

17. Glue the Desk Case Assembly to the Desk Leg Assembly. Center the Desk Leg Assembly on the Desk Case Floor.

Assembling the Desk Seat

18. Cut the Seat and the Seat Back pieces to the sizes specified on the materials list. Be certain the length of the Support Stretcher and the length of the Seat and Seat Back pieces are the same.

19. Round the edges of the Seat and the Seat Back. Use a file and a sanding block to round the edges. Do not round the ends of these pieces.

20. Glue and clamp the Seat, the Seat Back, and the Support Stretcher to the Seat Sides. Ensure the clamped assembly is square.

Finishing

21. Sand all of the wood surfaces.

22. Apply a stain and a finish to the Seat, the Seat Back, and the Desk Case Assembly.

23. Paint the Legs of the Desk and the Seat Assemblies with rusty brown acrylic craft paint.

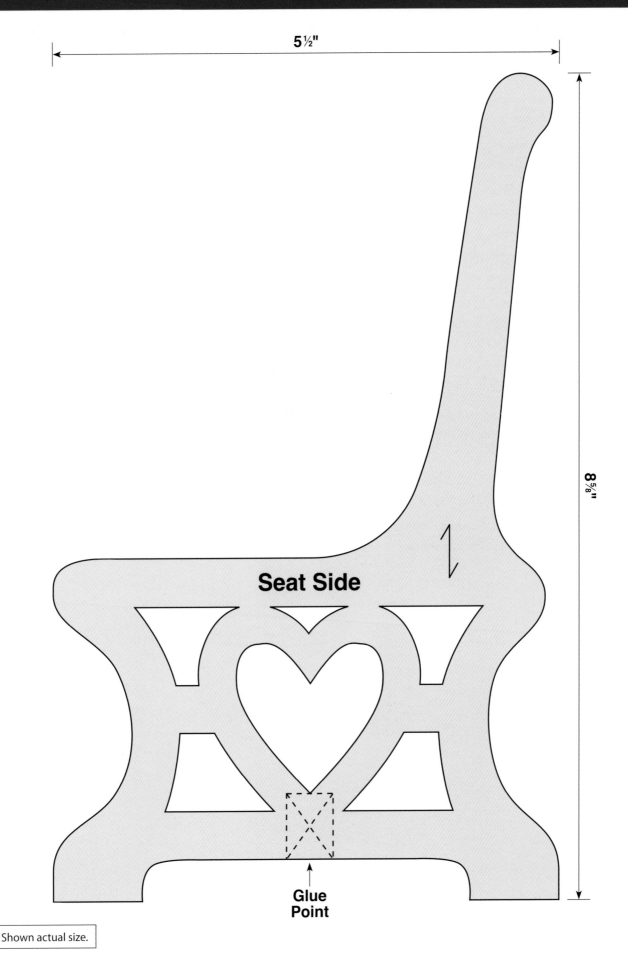

5½"

8⅝"

Seat Side

**Glue
Point**

Shown actual size.

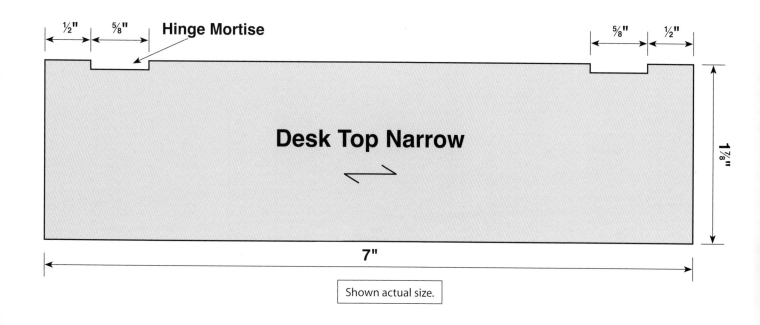

½"   ⅝"   **Hinge Mortise**   ⅝"   ½"

Desk Top Narrow

1⅞"

7"

Shown actual size.

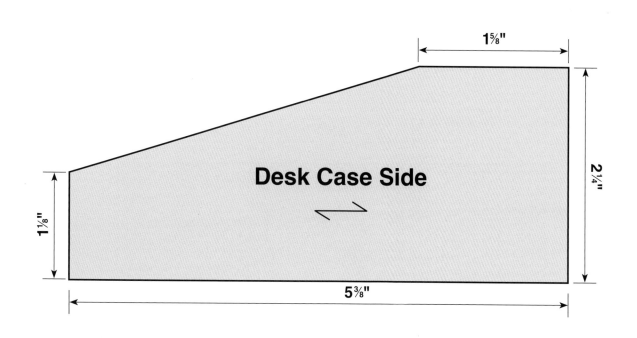

1⅝"

Desk Case Side

2¼"

1⅛"

5⅜"

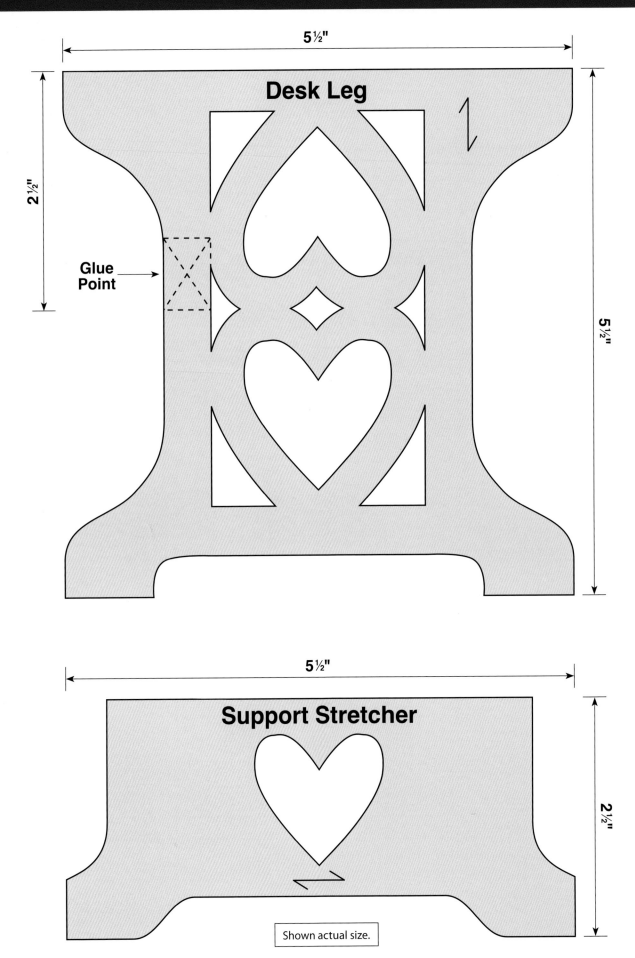

Desk Leg

5½"

2½"

5½"

Glue Point

1

Support Stretcher

5½"

2½"

Shown actual size.

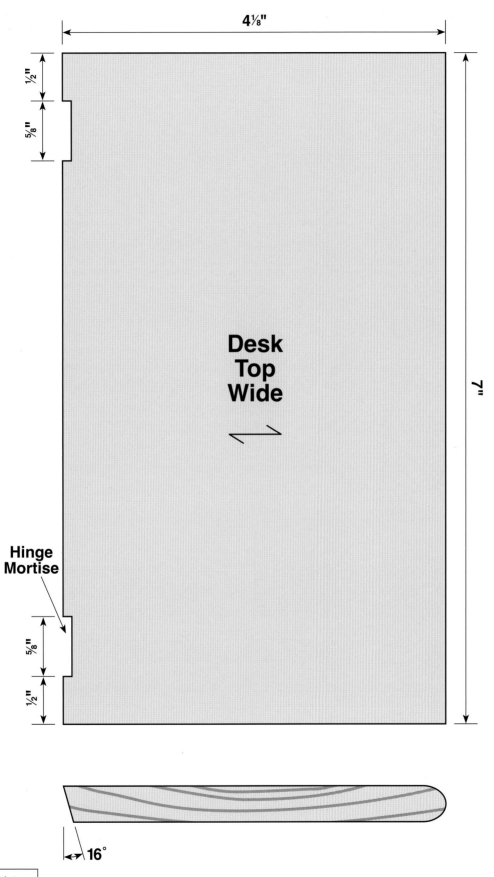

4⅛"

½"

⅝"

7"

**Desk
Top
Wide**

**Hinge
Mortise**

⅝"

½"

16°

Shown actual size.

Page 167

Page 174

Page 180

Storage Cases

As a final part in this book of doll furniture, I have included several items that are not necessarily furniture. However, these items can be made with all of the woodworking tools and techniques used in the previous chapters. They are storage cases, and they will help to keep any collector's—young and old alike—collection of dolls organized and securely stored when not on display or in use.

Here in this chapter you will find four storage cases designed especially for 18" dolls: the Hope Chest, Southwestern Trunk, Traveling Case, and Classic Trunk.

The box-making methods learned in the previous chapters will help you construct all of these projects. The Traveling Case requires the application of a heavy weight wall covering. The manufacturer's directions should be followed when gluing the paper onto the traveling case. A fabric material could be substituted for the wall covering if excessive handling is likely to occur.

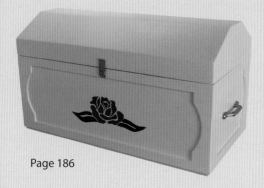

Page 186

Hope Chest

Materials List

Item	Width	Length	Thickness	Quantity	Material	Location
Bottom	12¾" (324mm)	23½" (597mm)	½" (13mm)	1	Walnut	No drawing
Decorative Piece	2¼" (57mm)	7" (178mm)	¼" (6mm)	1	Cherry	Page 169
End	11" (279mm)	12¾" (324mm)	½" (13mm)	2	Walnut	Page 170
Foot	3¼" (83mm)	3¼" (83mm)	¾" (19mm)	4	Walnut	Page 171
Front & Back	11" (279mm)	24" (610mm)	½" (13mm)	2	Walnut	Page 172
Hinge	1⅜" (35mm)	2" (51mm)		2	Hardware	No drawing
Lid Narrow	4" (102mm)	24¾" (629mm)	½" (13mm)	1	Walnut	No drawing
Lid Support		7" (178mm)		1	Hardware	No drawing
Lid Wide	9½" (241mm)	24¾" (629mm)	½" (13mm)	1	Walnut	No drawing
Splat	3" (76mm)	24" (610mm)	½" (13mm)	1	Walnut	Page 173

Making the Chest

1. Purchase ½"-thick walnut for this project.

2. Cut the Bottom and the End pieces to the sizes specified on the drawings and the materials list.

3. Cut a ½" x ¼" rabbet on all the edges of the End and the Front & Back pieces as specified on the drawings.

4. Apply glue to the rabbet cuts on the Front & Back pieces where the Ends will join. Clamp the assembly. Ensure the rabbet cuts in the End pieces are oriented in the same direction as the rabbet grooves on the Front & Back pieces. Ensure the assembly is square.

5. Cut the Bottom piece to the size specified on the materials list.

6. Apply glue to the rabbet cuts in the End and in the Front & Back pieces. Insert the Bottom piece and clamp the pieces to complete the assembly.

7. Select a ¾" board to be used to make the Foot pieces. Do not cut the Foot pieces to size yet. Cut a board that is 6½" x 6½" in size. Use a router with a ¼" Roman Ogee bit to cut the decorative edge on all of the edges of this board. Cut the Foot pieces to the dimensions indicated on the materials list.

8. Mark the locations on the Foot pieces where they will align with the corners of the Box Assembly. These will be set out from the corner ¾" on both edges. Apply glue to the Foot pieces and clamp them to the Box Assembly. Screws could be used to supplement this attachment, if desired.

9. Cut the Lid Wide and the Lid Narrow pieces to the sizes specified on the drawing and the materials list.

10. Measure and mark the location where the Lid Narrow will fit to the Box Assembly. This piece is flush with the Back and centered on the length of the Box Assembly.

11. Mark the locations along the joining edges and drill pilot holes for the 1¼" finishing brad nails. Use two on each end and three along the back.

> **Technical Note:**
> The Legs must remain attached to the wood pieces until after the mortises have been cut in the Leg pieces.

12. Apply glue on the top edge of the Box Assembly where these pieces will join. Attach the Lid Narrow to the Box Assembly using the brad nails. Clamp this assembly until the glue is dry. Use a nail set to countersink the nailheads below the wood surface. Use wood filler to hide these nailheads.

13. Select the wood to be used for the Splat. Ensure the edge of the board is straight. Use a wood plane or jointer to straighten this edge, if necessary.

14. Photocopy the pattern for the Splat. Use temporary adhesive to attach the photocopy to the Splat. Cut the profile using a scroll saw, band saw, or jigsaw.

15. Select the wood for the Decorative Piece. Photocopy the pattern for this piece. Use temporary adhesive to attach the photocopy to the Decorative Piece. Cut the profile using a scroll saw, band saw, or jigsaw.

16. Use a woodcarving gouge to cut the relief areas of the Decorative Piece to create the rising sun decoration. Sand and smooth all of the edges and grooves.

17. Mark the location on the Splat where the Decorative Piece will be attached. Apply glue to the backside of the Decorative Piece and clamp it to the Splat.

18. Mark the location where the Splat will be attached to the Lid Narrow. This will be inset from the back edge by ¾". Mark the location for the three screws, centered where the Splat will attach and spaced with one in the center and two others 7" out from the center.

19. Drill pilot holes for the #4 screws in the Lid Narrow and mating holes in the edge of the Splat.

20. Apply glue to the edge of the Splat and use 1"-long screws to attach it to the Top.

21. Lay the Lid Wide in place on the Box Assembly. Mark the location for the Hinges 4" in from each end. Drill pilot holes matching the Hinges. Attach the Hinges to complete the assembly of the hope chest. Install Lid Support hardware inside box if desired.

22. Sand the chest, inside and out, and apply a finish.

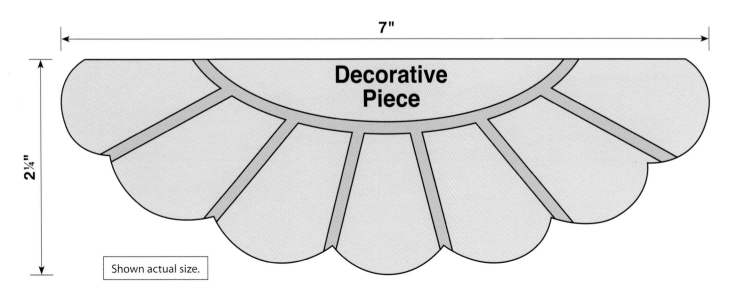

7"

2¼"

Decorative Piece

Shown actual size.

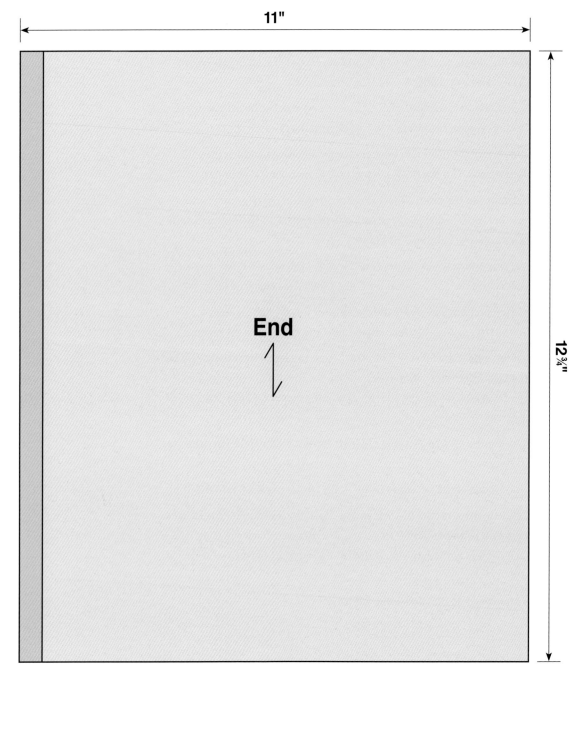

11"

12 ¾"

End

½"

¼"

½"

Enlarge 200% to
achieve actual size.

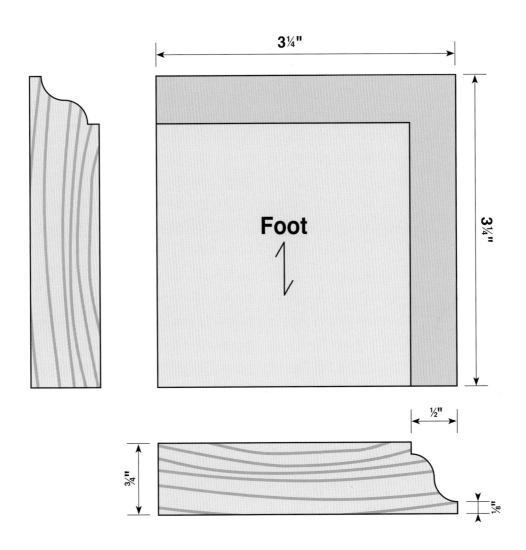

3¼"

3¼"

Foot

½"

3/4"

1/8"

Shown actual size.

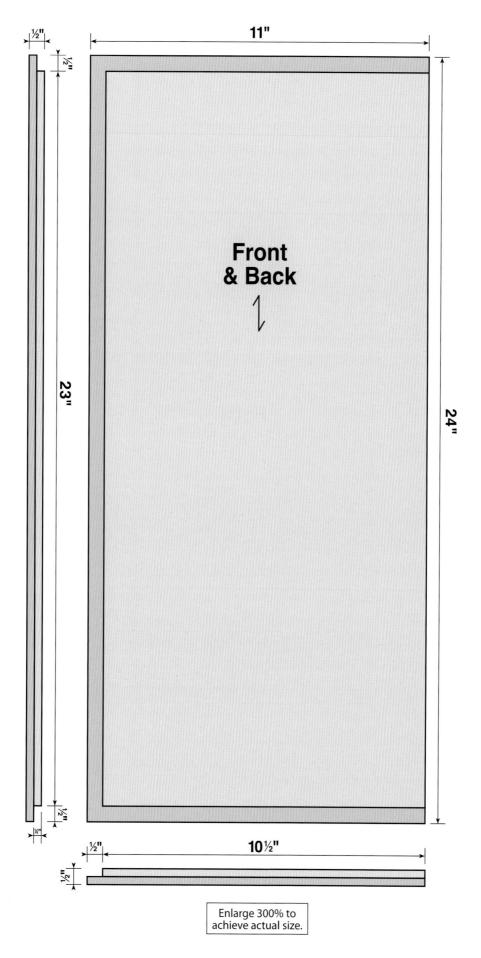

½"

½"

11"

23"

24"

**Front
& Back**

½"

¼"

½"

10½"

½"

½"

Enlarge 300% to
achieve actual size.

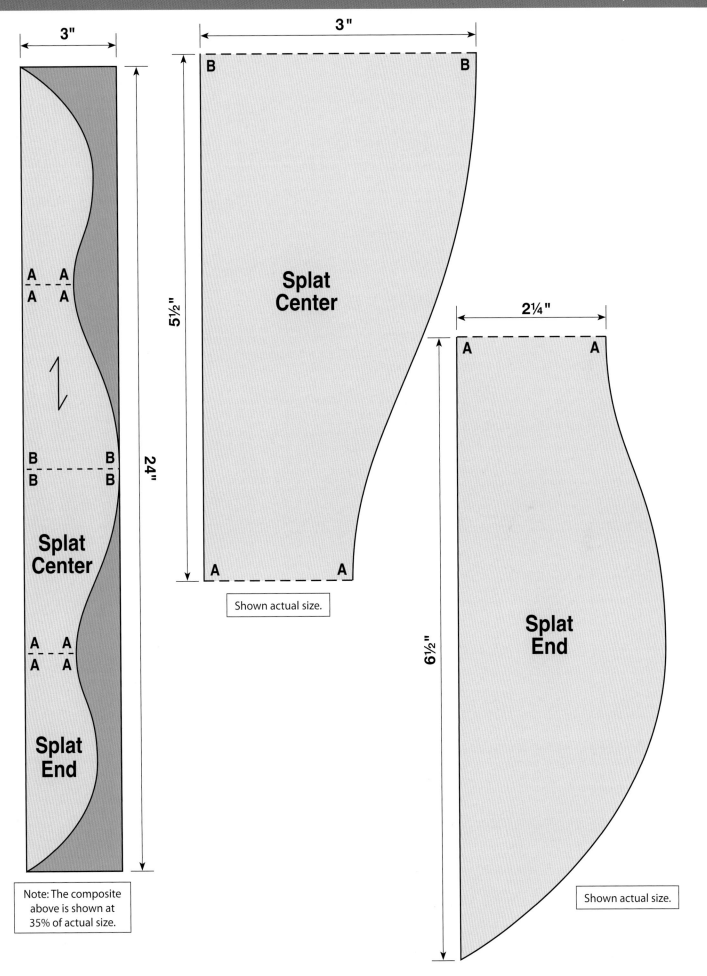

3"

5½"

3"

B   B

**Splat
Center**

A   A
A   A

2¼"

A   A

B   B
B   B

24"

**Splat
Center**

A   A

A   A
A   A

Shown actual size.

**Splat
End**

6½"

**Splat
End**

Note: The composite above is shown at 35% of actual size.

Shown actual size.

Southwestern Trunk

Materials List

Item	Width	Length	Thickness	Quantity	Material	Location
Corner Trim	1¼" (32mm)	335" (8509mm)	¼" (6mm)	1	Poplar	No drawing
Decorative Trim	5" (127mm)	18" (457mm)	¼" (6mm)	2	Poplar	Page 178
Diamond	5" (127mm)	7" (178mm)	¼" (6mm)	2	Poplar	Page 177
End	11" (279mm)	11¾" (298mm)	⅜" (10mm)	2	Plywood	No drawing
Front & Back	11" (279mm)	24¾" (629mm)	⅜" (10mm)	2	Plywood	No drawing
Handle		4" (102mm)		2	Hardware	No drawing
Lid Support		7" (178mm)		1	Hardware	No drawing
Notched Corner	3" (76mm)	3" (76mm)	¼" (6mm)	4	Poplar	Page 178
Rustic Hinge	1½" (38mm)	1½" (38mm)		2	Hardware	No drawing
Top & Bottom	12½" (318mm)	24¾" (629mm)	⅜" (10mm)	2	Plywood	Page 179

Making the Trunk

1. Purchase ⅜" A-C plywood for this project.

2. Cut the Top & Bottom pieces to the sizes specified on the drawing.

3. Cut a ⅜" x ³⁄₁₆" rabbet on all edges of the Top & Bottom piece as specified on the drawing.

4. Cut the Ends and the Front & Back pieces to the sizes specified on the materials list.

5. Apply glue to each end of the End pieces and clamp them to the Front & Back pieces. Ensure the assembly is square.

6. Apply glue to the rabbet cut in the Top & Bottom pieces and clamp these to the assembly to create a totally enclosed box.

7. Use ¼"-thick poplar to cut six Corner Trim pieces for the 24¾" length across the Front, the Back, and the Top.

8. Apply glue and use ½" brad nails to attach the Corner Trim pieces to the Box Assembly.

9. Cut six Corner Trim pieces for the 12½" Ends. Use glue and nails to attach them to the Box Assembly.

10. Cut eight Corner Trim pieces for the 10½" vertical corners of the Box Assembly. Use glue and nails to attach these to the Box Assembly.

11. Photocopy the pattern for the Notched Corner pieces. Use temporary adhesive to attach the photocopy to the wood selected for these pieces. Cut out the four Notched Corner pieces.

12. Apply glue and use ½" brad finish nails to attach these pieces to the corners of the Top.

13. Photocopy the pattern for the Decorative Trim. Use temporary adhesive to attach the photocopy to the wood selected for these pieces. Cut out the two Diamond pieces using a scroll saw or a band saw.

14. Apply glue and use ½" brad finish nails to attach these Diamond pieces in the center of each End.

15. Photocopy the pattern for the Diamond Trim. Use temporary adhesive to attach the photocopy to the wood selected for these pieces. Cut out the two Diamond Trim pieces using a scroll saw or a band saw.

16. Apply glue and use ½" brad finish nails to attach these Diamond Trim pieces in the center of the Top and the Front.

17. Use a woodcarving gouge to cut random grooves in the Notched Corner, the Diamond Trim, and the Decorative Trim pieces. This gives the wood a weathered, rustic look after a stain is applied.

18. Cut the Box Assembly to separate the lid from the remainder of the box. The lid thickness should be 1½". (Cut along the edge of the Corner Trim attached to the Front of the box.) This can be done using a table saw or jigsaw.

19. Cut one more Corner Trim piece 22¼" long. Apply glue and use ½" brad finish nails to attach this piece to the top edge of the Back.

20. Install two Rustic Hinges 3" from the ends to join the box to the lid.

21. Install two rustic drawer pulls to the Ends to use as Handles.

22. Install Lid Support hardware inside the box, if desired.

23. Sand the trunk inside and out and apply a stain and a finish.

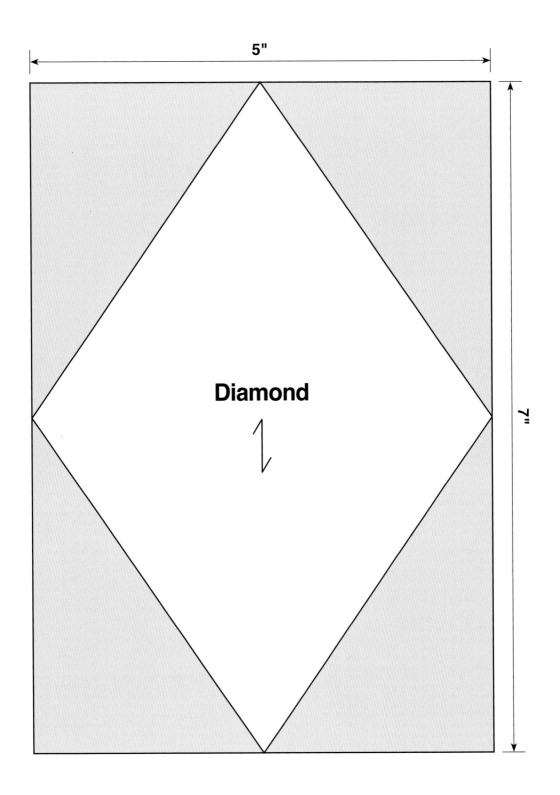

5"

7"

Diamond

Shown actual size.

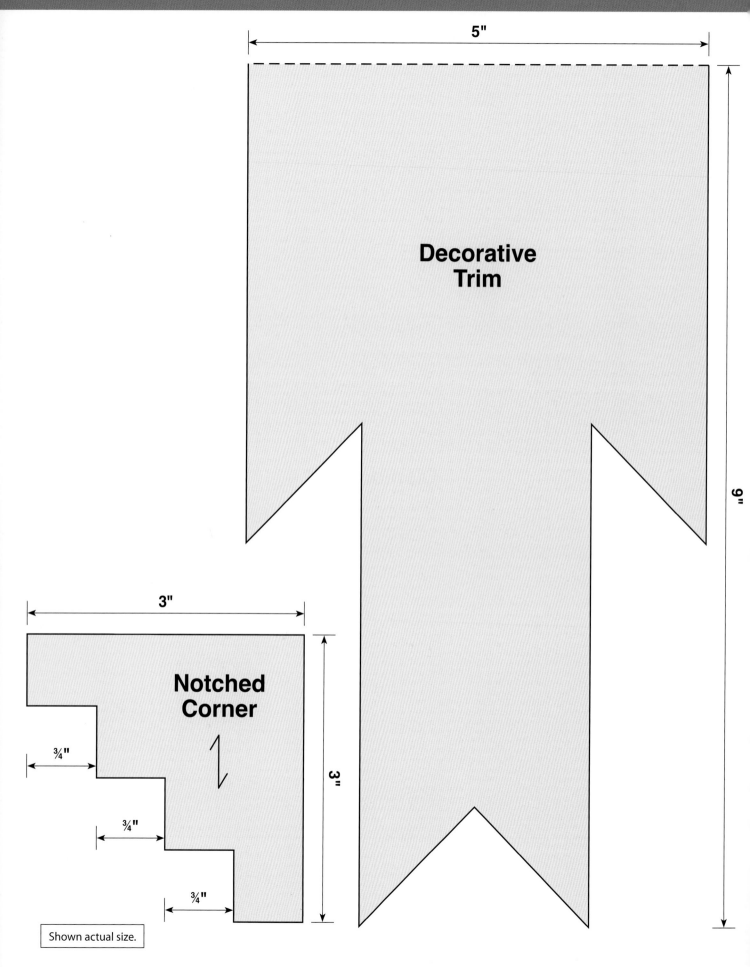

5"

**Decorative
Trim**

9"

3"

**Notched
Corner**

3"

¾"

¾"

¾"

Shown actual size.

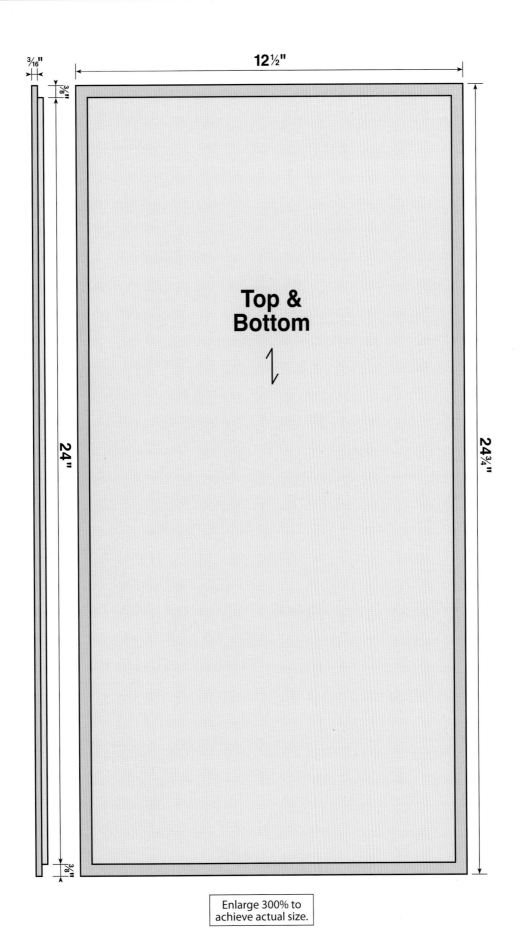

3/16"

3/8"

12½"

24"

24¾"

Top & Bottom

3/8"

Enlarge 300% to achieve actual size.

Traveling Case

Materials List

Item	Width	Length	Thickness	Quantity	Material	Location
Corner		1" (25mm)		8	Brass Hardware	No drawing
End	8" (203mm)	10" (254mm)	⅜" (10mm)	2	Plywood	Page 183
Handle		4" to 6" (102mm to 152mm)		1	Plastic	No drawing
Hanger		13" (330mm)		4	Soft wire	Page 182
Hanger Rod		7" (178mm)		1	Soft wire	Page 182
Hasp		2⅜" (60mm)		2	Brass Hardware	No drawing
Hinge		2½" (64mm)		2	Brass Hardware	No drawing
Side	8" (203mm)	19¾" (502mm)	⅜" (10mm)	2	Plywood	No drawing
Top & Bottom	10" (254mm)	20" (508mm)	⅜" (10mm)	2	Plywood	Page 184
Vinyl #1	24" (610mm)	34" (864mm)		2	Vinyl Wallpaper	Page 185
Vinyl #2	11" (279mm)	21" (533mm)		2	Vinyl Wallpaper	No drawing
Vinyl #3	3¾" (95mm)	60" (1524mm)		2	Vinyl Wallpaper	No drawing

Making the Traveling Case Assembly

1. Purchase ⅜" A-C plywood for this project.

2. Cut all of the plywood pieces to the sizes specified on the drawings and the materials list.

3. Cut a ⅜" x 1¼" rabbet on the Top & Bottom pieces as specified on the drawing.

4. Cut a ⅜" x ¼" rabbet on the 8" width for the Ends as specified on the drawing.

5. Dry fit all of the pieces for the box.

6. Apply glue to the rabbet cut in the Ends and clamp the Sides to the Ends. Ensure the assembly is square.

7. Apply glue to the rabbet cut in the Top & Bottom pieces and clamp the Top & Bottom pieces to the assembly to create a totally enclosed box.

8. Use a router with a pilot-guided ¼" round over bit on all edges of the Box Assembly.

9. Cut the assembly in two separate pieces, each being 4" tall.

Installing the Covering Material

10. Sand the Box Assembly, inside and out. Smooth all of the rounded edges and corners.

11. Apply a coat of primer to the Box Assembly, inside and out. Sand the primer after it dries and apply a second coat, if needed.

12. Purchase a single roll of heavy-duty vinyl wallpaper.

13. Coat the Box Assembly inside and out with wallpaper sizing.

14. Cut a section of wallpaper that will cover the Top, the Sides, and the Ends and extend 3" on the insides of these surfaces. Reference the measurement specified on the Vinyl #1 drawing.

> **Technical Note:**
> The primer is used to seal the wood to help the wallpaper adhere better.

15. Follow the wallpaper manufacturer's directions to wet and book the wallpaper.

16. Apply the wallpaper to the Box Assembly and smooth out the wrinkles. Because of the rounded corners, the wallpaper will not fit well in the corners. These corners will be covered later by the Corner pieces.

17. Cut a piece of wallpaper to cover the inside of the Top & Bottom pieces. This piece should be oversized to overlap the Sides. Reference the measurements specified on the Vinyl #2 drawing. Apply this piece, following the steps outlined above.

18. Cut a piece of wallpaper to cover the insides of the Sides. This band strip will cover the edges where the previous pieces ended. Reference the measurements specified on the Vinyl #3 drawing. Apply this piece, following the steps outlined above.

Installing the Hardware

19. Install the metal Corner protectors to all eight corners of the Box Assembly.

20. Install surface-mounted Hinges 3" in from the ends.

21. Install the Hasps on the front of the Box Assembly 3" in from the ends.

22. A Handle could be installed on one end of the Box Assembly, if desired.

23. The Hanger Rod is made using a piece of soft wire. Bend it to the size specified on the drawing. Twist the ends of the wire with needle-nose pliers to form a screw loop on each end.

24. Attach the Hanger Rod to the inside of the Box Assembly using ½"-long screws.

25. Wire Hangers may be made by following the drawing. Use a length of wire approximately 13" long for each Hanger.

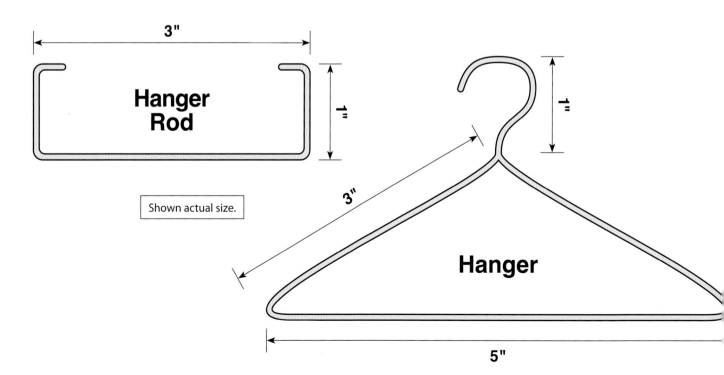

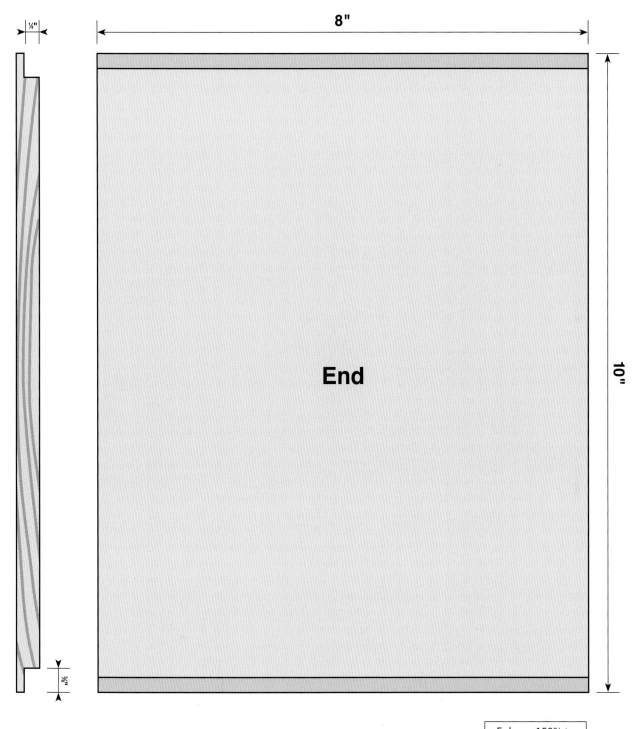

8"

¼"

10"

⅜"

End

Enlarge 150% to
achieve actual size.

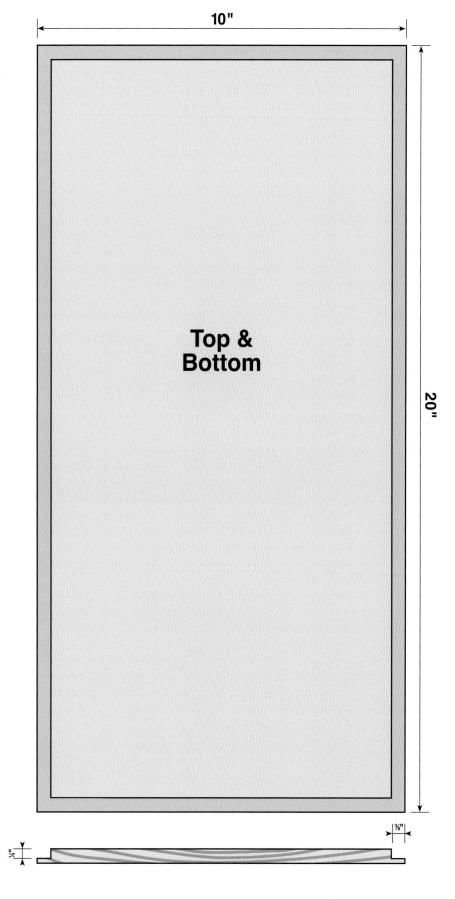

10"

20"

**Top &
Bottom**

⅜"

¼"

Enlarge 250% to
achieve actual size.

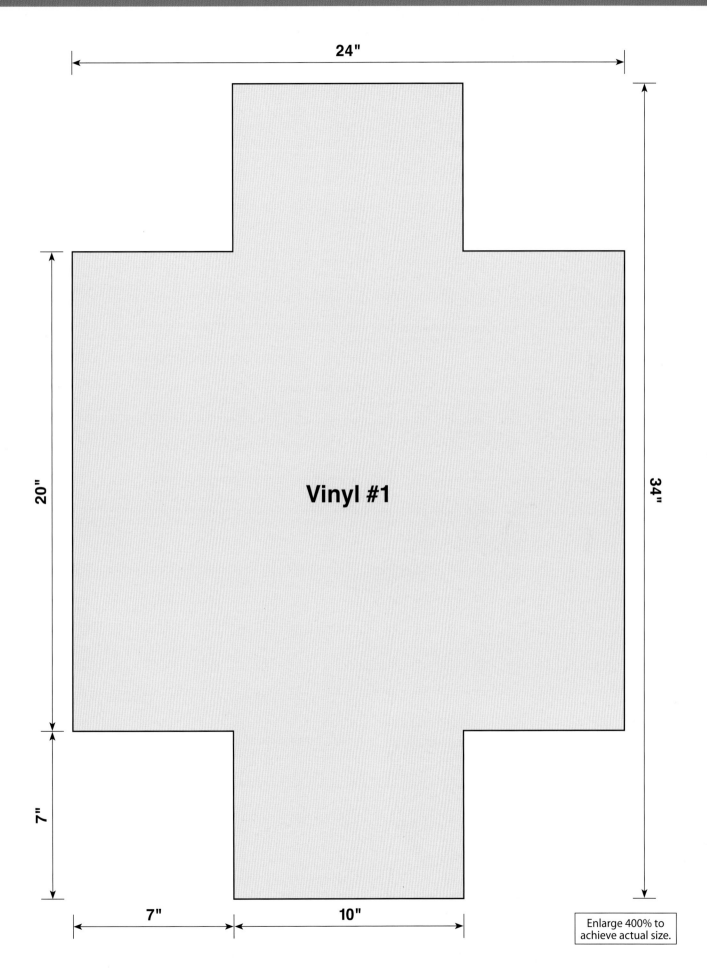

24"

20"

34"

7"

7"

10"

Vinyl #1

Enlarge 400% to
achieve actual size.

Classic Trunk

Materials List

Item	Width	Length	Thickness	Quantity	Material	Location
Bottom	13" (330mm)	24½" (622mm)	⅜" (10mm)	1	Plywood	No drawing
Corner Trim	2" (51mm)	6½" (165mm)	¼" (6mm)	8	Pine or Poplar	Page 190
Edge Trim	1¼" (32mm)	150" (3810m)	¼" (6mm)	1	Pine or Poplar	No drawing
End	9" (229mm)	12¼" (311mm)	⅜" (10mm)	2	Plywood	No drawing
Front & Back	9" (229mm)	24½" (622mm)	⅜" (10mm)	2	Plywood	No drawing
Handle		4" (102mm)		2	Brass Hardware	No drawing
Hasp	1" (25mm)	2" (51mm)		1	Brass Hardware	No drawing
Hinge	1⅜" (35mm)	2" (51mm)		2	Brass Hardware	No drawing
Lid Angle Slat	5¾" (146mm)	24½" (622mm)	½" (13mm)	2	Pine or Poplar	Page 193
Lid End	4⅛" (105mm)	14¼" (362mm)	½" (13mm)	2	Pine or Poplar	Page 191
Lid Front & Back	2" (51mm)	24½" (622mm)	½" (13mm)	2	Pine or Poplar	Page 190
Lid Rib	4⅜" (111mm)	13¼" (337mm)	½" (13mm)	2	Pine or Poplar	Page 194
Lid Support		7" (178mm)		1	Hardware	No drawing
Lid Top Slat	4¼" (108mm)	24½" (622mm)	½" (13mm)	1	Pine or Poplar	Page 193
Tray Bottom	11⅜" (289mm)	22⅞" (581mm)	¼" (6mm)	1	Plywood	No drawing
Tray End	4¼" (108mm)	10⅞" (276mm)	½" (13mm)	2	Pine or Poplar	Page 192
Tray Side	3" (76mm)	23⅜" (594mm)	½" (13mm)	2	Pine or Poplar	Page 192
Tray Support	1¼" (32mm)	12¼" (311mm)	¾" (19mm)	2	Pine or Poplar	Page 194

Making the Box Assembly

1. Cut the plywood materials to the sizes specified on the materials list for the Bottom, the Front & Back, and the Ends.

2. Cut a ⅜" x ¼" rabbet on all edges of the Bottom.

3. Apply glue to the rabbets in the Bottom piece and to each end of the Ends.

4. Clamp the Ends to the Front & Back and Bottom pieces to make the Box Assembly. Ensure the assembly is square.

5. Rip cut 150" of ¼"-thick wood to a width of 1¼" for the Edge Trim.

6. Cut four pieces of the Edge Trim materials 24½" long.

7. Apply glue and use ½"-long brad finish nails to attach two of the Edge Trim pieces flush with the top edge on the Front & Back of the Box Assembly.

8. Cut four Edge Trim pieces 13" long for the Ends.

9. Apply glue and use ½"-long brad finish nails to attach two of the Edge Trim pieces to the top edge on the Ends.

10. Photocopy the pattern for the Corner Trim pieces. Use temporary adhesive to attach the photocopy to a scrap piece of ¼" plywood. Cut a wood template for the Corner Trim pieces.

11. Use the wood template to lay out and cut eight Corner Trim pieces.

12. Apply glue and use ½"-long brad finish nails to attach four of the Corner Trim pieces to the Ends. Be certain the Corner Trim pieces are flush with the Front & Back respectively.

13. Apply glue and use ½"-long brad finish nails to attach the remaining four Corner Trim pieces to the corners on the Front & Back. Ensure the Corner Trim pieces are flush with the Corner Trim pieces installed in the previous step.

14. Apply glue and use ½"-long brad finish nails to attach the remaining Edge Trim pieces to the bottom edge of the Front & Back and the Ends respectively.

Making the Lid Assembly

15. Cut the materials for the Lid Ends using ⅜" wood.

16. Cut a ½" x ¼" rabbet on the edges of the Lid Ends as specified on the drawing.

17. Cut two Lid Ribs to the size specified on the drawing.

18. Cut two pieces for the Lid Front & Back pieces.

19. Cut a ½" x ¼" rabbet on one edge of each Lid Front & Back piece as specified on the drawing.

20. Cut one Lid Top Slat and two Lid Angle Slats to the sizes specified on the drawing.

21. Cut 75° miters on the edges of the Lid Top and the Angle Slats.

22. Dry assemble the Lid Assembly to ensure a good fit at all connecting points. Confirm that the overall size is 25" long x 13½" wide. Confirm the size matches the overall size of the Box Assembly as measured in the technical note above.

23. Apply glue to the rabbet where the Lid Front attaches to the Lid Ends. Use 1¼"-long brad finish nails to attach the Lid Front & Back pieces to the Lid Ends. Be certain the rabbet cuts in the Lid Front & Back pieces are oriented up and facing toward the inside of the trunk lid.

24. Measure and mark the location where the Lid Ribs will attach to the Lid Front & Back pieces. The Lid Ribs are located 8" in from each end.

25. Apply glue and attach the Lid Ribs to the Lid Assembly using 1¼"-long brad finish nails. Ensure the Lid Ribs are square with the Lid Assembly and the top edge is flush with the rabbets on the Lid Ends.

26. Apply glue to the rabbet areas in the Lid Front piece and Lid End where the Lid Angle Slat will attach. Use 1¼"-long brad finish nails to attach the Lid Angle Slat to the Lid Assembly.

27. Follow this same procedure to attach the other Lid Angle Slat to the Lid Assembly.

28. Check the fit of the Lid Top Slat with the Lid Angle Slats. Adjust the width, if necessary, to accomplish a tight-fitting joint.

Technical Note:
The overall size of the Box Assembly should be 25" long x 13½" wide and 9" high. If your results are different, please note this difference. Changes will need to be made to the overall size when making the Lid Assembly.

29. Apply glue to the mitered edges of the Lid Top Slat and all of the contact areas with the Lid Assembly. Use 1¼"-long brad finish nails to attach this Lid Top Slat to the Lid Assembly.

30. Use a nail set to recess the brad nails below the wood surface. Use wood filler to fill the nail holes.

Making the Tray Assembly

31. The finished tray size will be 11⅞" x 23⅜". Confirm the size matches the overall size of the Box Assembly measured in the technical note on page 188.

32. Cut a piece of wood 22" long for the Tray Ends.

33. Cut a piece of wood 47" long for the Tray Sides.

34. Cut a ¼" x 1¼" dado groove in the Tray Ends and in the Tray Sides as specified on the drawings.

35. Cut a piece of ¼" plywood for the Tray Bottom.

36. Cut the Tray Sides to the length specified on the drawing.

37. Cut the Tray Ends to the length specified on the drawing.

38. Photocopy the drawing for the Tray Ends. Use temporary adhesive to attach the photocopy to the wood pieces for the Tray Ends.

39. Drill pilot holes for the Handle holes. Cut the Handle holes and the angle cuts on the Tray Ends.

40. Apply glue to both ends of the Tray Ends and to the dado grooves in all of the pieces. Use 1¼"-long brad finish nails to attach the Tray Front to the Tray Ends.

41. Cut two Tray Support pieces to ¾" x 1¼" x 12¼" long. Attach the Tray Supports inside the trunk Ends, using glue and 1"-long brad finish nails. Align these Tray Supports 2¾" down from the top edge of the Box Assembly.

Attaching the Lid to the Trunk Assembly

42. Mark the location for the Hinges 4" in from the Ends. Drill pilot holes for the screws and attach the Hinges using the screws.

43. Mount the Lid Support to the inside of the lid and attach the Handles to the Ends.

44. Install the Hasp or trunk latches available from your local hardware supplier.

45. Sand the trunk and apply a finish.

46. Stencils are available from your local arts and crafts suppliers.

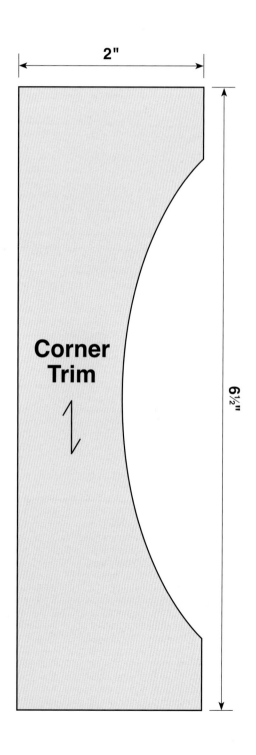

2"

Corner
Trim

6½"

2"

Lid
Front
& Back

Extend to 24½"

½"

¼"

Shown actual size.

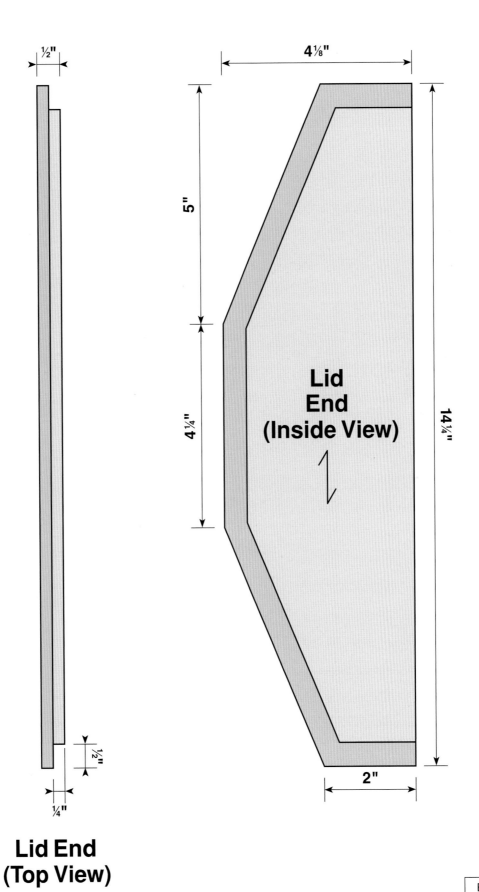

½"

4⅛"

5"

4¼"

14¼"

**Lid
End
(Inside View)**

2"

½"

¼"

**Lid End
(Top View)**

Enlarge 200% to
achieve actual size.

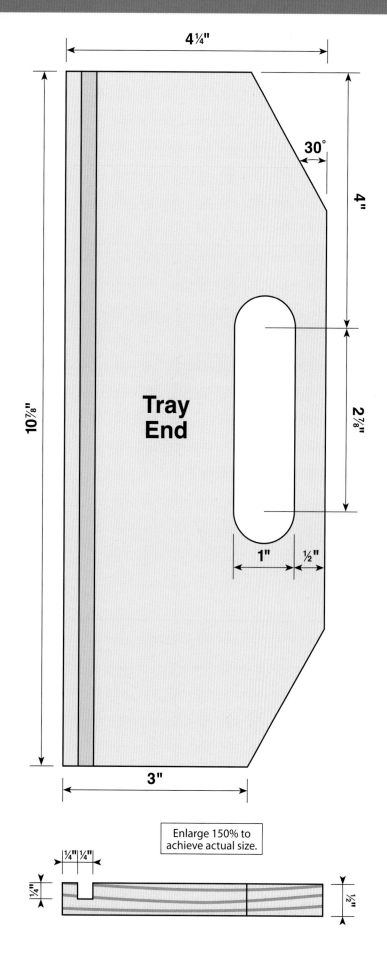

Tray End

Enlarge 150% to achieve actual size.

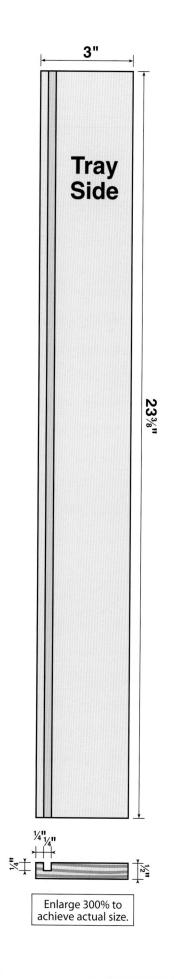

Tray Side

Enlarge 300% to achieve actual size.

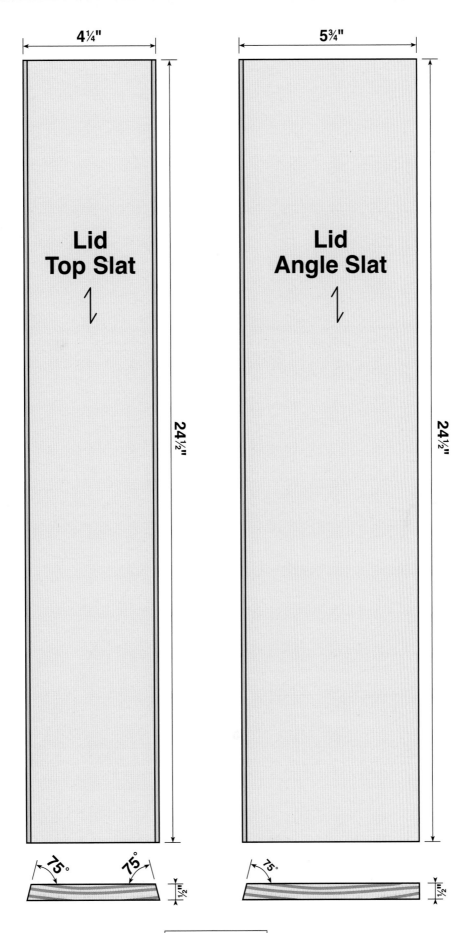

4¼"

5¾"

**Lid
Top Slat**

**Lid
Angle Slat**

24½"

24½"

75° 75°

75°

½"

½"

Enlarge 300% to
achieve actual size.

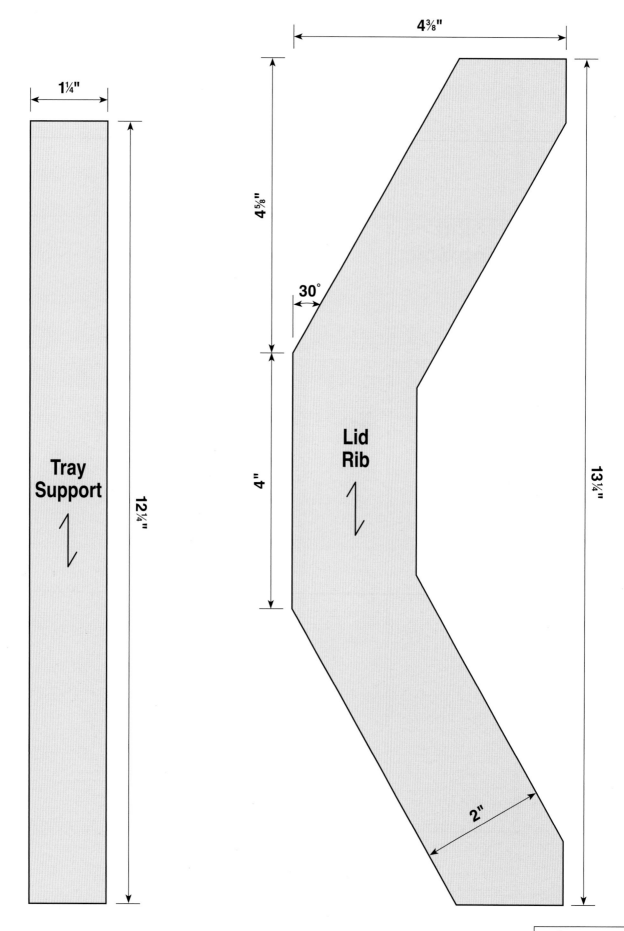

Tray Support

Lid Rib

1¼"

12¼"

4⅜"

4⅝"

30°

4"

13¼"

2"

Enlarge 150% to achieve actual size.

Appendix: Materials and Techniques

There are a number of points a woodworker needs to keep in mind when making wooden furniture for dolls. This chapter will provide instruction and insight on the basics.

Recommended tools

All of the projects in this book were made using common woodworking tools. You will need the following basic tools to make doll furniture. Certain projects in this book may require additional tools.

Power tools

Scroll saw

Band saw

Table saw

Miter saw

Router

Drill press with mortise attachment

Jointer

Thickness planer

Hand tools

Steel square, 3"-6" (76mm-152mm)

Small-sized bar clamps

Steel scale, 6" (152mm)

Calipers, 6"-8" (152mm-203mm)

Mini bench vise (optional)

Along with a sharpened pencil and measuring devices, you will need a depth gauge (in my hand) a caliper (bottom right) and a combination square (bottom left).

Patterns and drawings

Drawings are provided for each individual furniture part needed to make the projects. Some drawings have side views or end views; others do not. Side or end views are provided only when the piece has a special feature that needs additional explanation. Drawings are not provided for simple rectangular parts. Measurement for these parts are included in the materials list. Drawings have been made full-size when possible. Some full-sized drawings have a section removed (indicated by a wavy line). This technique permits those drawings to fit on the printed page. Other drawings that could not fit on the printed page have been reduced to permit the entire part to be shown. These drawings can be enlarged with the aid of a photocopy machine to create the full-sized patterns. The percentage for enlargement appears on the drawing. A symbol is used near the drawing name on each drawing to indicate the recommended direction of the wood grain.

Notice how the narrow grain pattern in the wood on this Adirondack chair gives the chair an authentic look. Wood with a wider grain pattern would give the chair an odd appearance.

Some of the furniture pieces in this book have decorative, curved shapes that are difficult to dimension. This problem can easily be resolved. Full-sized paper patterns of any piece can be made using a photocopy machine. The photocopy paper pattern can then be attached to the wood piece using a temporary adhesive. Follow the lines on the paper pattern when cutting the decorative shape. Temporary mounting adhesives are available from arts and crafts stores and office supply stores.

Sawing a board through its thickness will result in two or more thinner boards. This technique is called re-sawing and is useful in creating the thinner boards needed for doll furniture construction.

Smoothing boards that have been re-sawn is a necessity and can be done with a thickness planer, as shown here, or with a jointer.

Wood selection

Fine-grained hardwood is recommended for the doll furniture pieces. Clear, straight-grained boards should be selected. Boards normally have variations in grain line width. The wider grain pattern sections normally found in boards are out-of-scale when making miniature furniture. When making doll furniture, strive to choose boards or sections of boards with the narrowest grain lines possible. The narrower the grain lines, the more authentic the finished furniture piece will look.

Authentic wood panels

Cabinet sides, tabletops, and chair seats are examples of full-sized furniture pieces that are made from wide wood panels. Wide wood panels are made from several boards glued together to form a larger panel. Gluing boards together in full-sized furniture is a must because wide boards are not available. However, gluing boards together when making doll furniture is optional.

To make doll furniture look authentic, glue narrow boards together to form larger panels. Plywood can be used when making panels to simplify construction.

Making thin wood

The doll furniture projects in this book require the use of wood ranging from ⅛" – ¾" thick. Thin wood can be purchased at specialty wood supply stores or by mail order. Check the yellow pages of your local phone book or do an Internet search to find suppliers.

Standard ¾" and 1½" thick boards can be cut into thinner boards using a technique called re-sawing. Re-sawing refers to cutting a board through the thickness into two or more thinner boards. Re-sawing is most often done using a band saw or a table saw. Narrower width boards, 1½" or less, can be re-sawn on a scroll saw. The thin boards cut by re-sawing will require the use of a thickness planer or jointer to remove saw blade marks and to ensure a consistent thickness.

Recommended fasteners

For safety reasons avoid using metal fasteners. If the furniture piece becomes broken through play or by accident, a child could be injured on a sharp metal fastener. Well-constructed glue joints are stronger than the wood itself and often need no additional fastener. Yellow wood glue was my glue of choice for all of the projects in this book. A small artist paintbrush may be used to apply glue to small parts. Excess wood glue should be promptly removed from areas where a finish will be applied.

Recommended hardware

The materials list for each project includes the recommended size for the hardware items required to make that particular project. Miniature hinges and screws are available but are more difficult to find. All hardware items used in this book were purchased from mail order suppliers.

Safety

Safety is the responsibility of the craftsperson using the tools. This book is not intended to teach the proper or safe usage of any tools mentioned. It is the responsibility of the craftsperson to read and follow all safety information provided with any tools used. Some photos in this book show power tools with safety guards removed to provide a clear view for photography. When working with power tools in your shop, use guards and manufacturer-recommended safety gear at all times.

Cutting small pieces of wood with power tools can be dangerous if not done properly. When possible, cut rabbets, dados, and miters before removing the small piece of furniture from the larger board.

Accuracy

Accurate measurements and precise cutting are required when making smaller projects like doll furniture. An inexpensive pair of calipers is helpful when measuring small pieces. Calipers can be used to measure outside dimensions, inside dimensions, and depths.

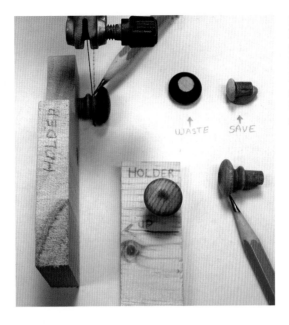

Doll furniture–sized pull knobs are easily made from small purchased knobs. Make a fixture to hold the knob by drilling a hole that matches the knob stem in a piece of scrap wood.

Making drawer pull knobs

Pull knobs of appropriate size for doll furniture are not available. Small wooden knobs may be modified easily. Use a simple fixture to hold the knob and cut the large end off. Sand and round the end of the new knob.

Finishing

Wipe-on polyurethane finish was used on the varnished projects in this book. Danish oil or tung oil will also work well. If child safety is a great concern, use finishes formulated for use on food containers such as toy and salad bowl finish. Non-toxic acrylic paints were used on the painted projects in this book.

Box-making

I like to glue boxes together as one unit and then cut it into two pieces. It is easier to glue and clamp a closed box than it is to make a separate lid and box and have them fit well, but either way will work. I use a table saw to cut the box in half. Set the blade to cut through one thickness of the wood and flip the box three times to cut all the sides. Any unsquareness that occurs will be in both halves, so the pieces will still fit together.

An easy joint, the butt joint is made by gluing the edge of one board to the flat surface of a second board.

Clamps are used to hold an edge joint as the glue dries.

A table-mounted router or a table saw can be used to cut a dado, which is a three-sided cut that joins two boards.

Wood joint primer

Several wood joints are used repeatedly throughout the projects in this book. Below is a quick look at these joints. If you are a beginning woodworker, refer to books on the subject of joints or take a class at a local woodworking store. It is imperative you understand these joints and how to use the tools that create them before you begin the projects in this book.

Butt joint

A butt joint is one of the easiest joints to make. The square end of one board is joined with a flat surface on the second board. The joint is held together with glue when making doll furniture.

Edge joint

When two or more boards are placed edge to edge and glued together to make a wider board, this is called an edge joint. The edges of the boards to be joined need to be straight and square with the face. The edges should be smoothed using a hand plane or power jointer. Use glue and bar clamps or pipe clamps to hold the boards in alignment until the glue dries.

Dado joint

A dado joint consists of a three-sided groove cut in the face of the first board and to a depth of one-fourth to one-half the thickness of the first board. The width of the groove is usually equal to the thickness of the second board. A dado groove can be cut using a table-mounted router or table saw.

Rabbet joint

A rabbet joint requires an L-shaped groove to be cut across the end or edge of the first board. The groove is usually cut into the first board to one-half to two-thirds of the first board's thickness. The groove width is equal to the thickness of the second board to be joined. A rabbet groove can be cut using a router or table saw.

Miter joint

A miter joint joins two pieces of wood cut at complementary angles. Both boards to be joined have an angle cut on mating surfaces. The angle is usually one-half of the total angle of the finished joint. For example, a 90° corner would require miter cuts of 45°. A flat miter joint is commonly seen in picture frames to hide end grain. An edge miter joint is used to hide end grain when making boxes. This joint is used in the treasure box project.

Mortise-and-tenon joint

This joint is a square or rectangular peg cut on the end of the first piece to be joined. A mating square or rectangular hole is cut into the face of the second piece to be joined. The mortise is cut using a mortise attachment on a drill press or a mortising machine. The tenon can be cut using a table router, band saw, or scroll saw. This joint is used in the bed, chest, and chair sections of this book.

The L-shaped cut of a rabbet joint can be cut with a router or table saw.

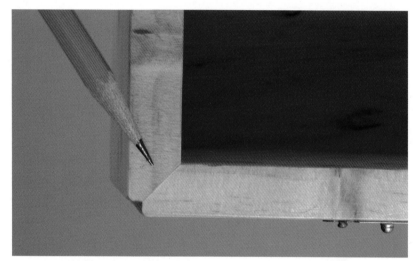

A miter joint joins two angled pieces of wood.

The tenon of a mortise-and-tenon joint can be cut on a scroll saw.

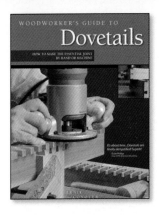

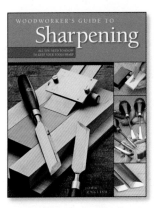
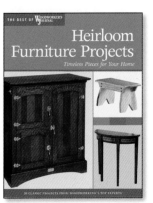
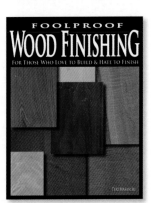